Exceeding
Customer
Expectations

Exceeding *Customer* Expectations

What Enterprise, America's #1 Car Rental Company, Can Teach You About Creating Lifetime Customers

Kirk Kazanjian

Foreword by ANDREW C. TAYLOR
Chairman and CEO, Enterprise Rent-A-Car

CURRENCY
DOUBLEDAY

NEW YORK LONDON TORONTO SYDNEY AUCKLAND

A CURRENCY BOOK
PUBLISHED BY DOUBLEDAY

Copyright © 2007 by Literary Productions

All Rights Reserved

Published in the United States by Doubleday, an imprint of The Doubleday
Broadway Publishing Group, a division of Random House, Inc., New York.
www.currencybooks.com

CURRENCY is a trademark of Random House, Inc., and DOUBLEDAY is a registered
trademark of Random House, Inc.

All trademarks are the property of their respective companies.

Book design by Chris Welch

Library of Congress Cataloging-in-Publication Data

Kazanjian, Kirk.
Exceeding customer expectations : what Enterprise, America's #1 car rental
company, can teach you about creating lifetime customers / Kirk Kazanjian ;
foreword by Andrew C. Taylor. — 1st ed.
p. cm.
Includes index.
1. Customer services—United States. 2. Enterprise Rent-A-Car.
I. Kazanjian, Kirk. II. Title.

HF5415.5.K388 2007
658.8'12—dc22

2006048969

ISBN-13: 978-0-385-51832-1
ISBN-10: 0-385-51832-3

PRINTED IN THE UNITED STATES OF AMERICA

SPECIAL SALES
Currency Books are available at special discounts for bulk purchases for sales
promotions or premiums. Special editions, including personalized covers, excerpts
of existing books, and corporate imprints, can be created in large quantities for
special needs. For more information, write to Special Markets, Currency Books,
specialmarkets@randomhouse.com

5 7 9 10 8 6 4

First Edition

Contents

Foreword

FIFTY YEARS AGO, when my dad leased his first brand-new Chevy Bel Air to a customer, he had no idea his start-up business would one day be the largest car rental company in North America, and arguably the world. In fact, becoming a *big* company was never his goal. His plan for success was to focus on a commonsense business approach: Treat your customers well, and give your employees respect and opportunities to grow. You know what? We found that when we did those things consistently, profits and growth naturally followed.

Sounds simple, and it is. But it works *very* well. By taking exceptionally good care of customers, you earn their steadfast loyalty. They pay us back by doing business with us over and over again. At the same time, by treating employees like owners and offering them great opportunities—professionally *and* financially—we not only encourage them to keep customers happy, we give them a powerful incentive to grow the business beyond everyone's wildest expectations.

I know a lot of businesses say they are committed to satisfying customers and developing their employees. But, at Enterprise, we have been fortunate enough to discover some tangible and effective ways to deliver on those commitments. As a result, we have built a successful, fast-growing company, while consistently earning high marks for excellent customer service.

Kirk Kazanjian took an interest in our company's story and thought our operating principles would be worth sharing with you. The result is this insightful book, *Exceeding Customer Expectations,* which has done an exceptional job of capturing what we like to call "The Enterprise Way." You'll discover how the unique manner in which we run our business has evolved into a winning formula for earning loyal customers, developing and motivating committed employees, and building a sustainable competitive advantage.

These are principles we have learned and refined over the past five decades. We know they work for us, but I believe they can work for you, too. After all, regardless of the product or service you sell, your customers and employees all want pretty much the same things.

I have had the privilege of leading the Enterprise Rent-A-Car team for more than twenty-five years. I am proud to say I had a great teacher—my father, Jack Taylor. Jack was a full-fledged member of the group we now fondly refer to as "The Greatest Generation." A decorated Navy fighter pilot in World War II, he spent part of his tour of duty flying off the aircraft carrier USS Enterprise. That is how our company got its name.

After the war, my father set aside his military accomplishments, returned home, and went to work building a business. He made it a rule early on that he would always enjoy his customers and associates, and he set out to ensure that everyone around him was having fun. In fact, to this day, the first thing he asks when talking with Enterprise employees is, "Are you having fun?"

Jack also discovered that you often uncover your best opportunities for success by listening to your customers. In the beginning, in fact, he did not set out to build a rental car company. Enterprise began as an automobile leasing business with a different name. But over time, his leasing customers would ask for loaner cars while their vehicles were in the shop. Jack listened. And he responded by offering daily rentals.

As it turned out, we wound up creating a whole new segment in the rental industry—convenient, affordable rentals right in the towns and neighborhoods where people live and work. We call it the home-city market, and today it makes up more than half of the nearly $20 billion car rental industry in the United States. We did not get to this point by hiring expensive consultants to map our course. We just developed a passion for nurturing close and enjoyable relationships with our customers, and cultivated a workplace environment in which employees enjoy their colleagues and their work, and are well rewarded for their efforts.

Another valuable lesson we have learned is just how important teamwork is to your success. I go to work every day knowing that I am supported by more than 62,000 incredibly hardworking and dynamic people. Our company would not be the success it is without a culture that treats teamwork as a sacred principle. Each of our nearly 7,000 branches operates as a team. We work and win together, and we reward hard work unlike most other companies in any industry. Indeed, I do not know of any company with a compensation and operational structure quite like ours. We provide tremendous upside potential for our employees, and we tie career advancement directly to how well our folks take care of our customers. After all, we want employees to go beyond just satisfying customers. We want them to exceed every customer's expectations. That is job number one at Enterprise. If you do not make that happen, you do not get promoted. It is that simple.

Teamwork is not just useful as an internal growth strategy. We have learned that it also pays big dividends when you develop important relationships outside of your company. Nothing illustrates this point better than the productive partnerships Enterprise has with the country's top insurance companies. Unlike other major rental car companies, our rental business did not begin at the airport. In fact, while the other players were busy building their businesses beside the nation's runways, we focused instead on the nation's driveways. We carved out our own niche—renting cars to people in their hometowns for a variety of purposes. One of the primary reasons folks need to rent a car locally is that their own vehicles are in the shop following an accident. So, for many years, we have teamed up with insurance companies to make the whole process as seamless as possible for all parties involved.

Teamwork in these business relationships means we work diligently to ensure that our business partners and the customers they entrust to us are treated exceptionally well, and we do everything possible to continually give them new, value-added services. In fact, we even came up with proprietary technology to help our insurance partners *reduce* the number of days a rental car is needed following an accident. You might not think that makes much business sense, since it results in less money per rental for us. But the opposite has been true. When we save our partners money, they bring us more business and our revenues continue to rise.

As I see it, building a successful company with satisfied customers comes down to understanding your strengths and capitalizing on them. Several years ago, I had a chance to meet with

EDS founder H. Ross Perot, who knows a thing or two about building a successful business. After hearing about the path we have taken at Enterprise, he looked at me and said, "Andy, you should be a Rhodes Scholar, only you should spell it R-O-A-D-S." He really liked our street-smart approach, including the way we refuse to give up on exceeding customer expectations, even when faced with tough roadblocks.

Like any other company, we have made missteps along the way. But we have learned through all of them. We have learned we cannot be all things to all people, and we are okay with that. Instead, we stay on target and focus on what we do best. It's worked well for us.

My father followed this advice better than anyone. When he was young, he was never a straight-A student. But he knew how people wanted to be treated. He had an inherent sense of how to run a business that he never learned in the classroom. He knew his own strengths and weaknesses, and tenaciously built this company around them. He was a true ROADS scholar.

This book is an opportunity for others to learn from our experiences. *Exceeding Customer Expectations* is about building a customer-centered business with a dedicated and motivated workforce that is absolutely passionate about seeing their business prosper. It is about finding ways to stand apart from the crowd, even in today's highly competitive marketplace, by focusing on areas that others have ignored. And it is about forming strong business partnerships that can help to propel your business forward.

The lessons and strategies outlined in this book have enabled my father's little start-up to grow into a multibillion-dollar, industry-leading company with tens of thousands of satisfied employees and millions of loyal customers. I hope you see ways to apply some of our hard-earned learning to your own business, and that these lessons bring you as much success and satisfaction as they have brought to the Enterprise family.

Andrew C. Taylor
Chairman and Chief Executive Officer
Enterprise Rent-A-Car

Introduction

WHAT BEGAN IN the basement of a Missouri Cadillac dealership some fifty years ago has evolved into one of the greatest modern-day examples of how to deliver excellent customer service while building an incredibly successful business.

As many of its competitors struggled with declining business, lost market share, and various other financial woes, Enterprise Rent-A-Car quietly grew into the largest and most successful car rental company in America and, by most measures, the world. From an initial investment of $100,000 and just seven cars, Enterprise has become a $9 billion global powerhouse with some 62,000 employees, nearly 7,000 locations, and a combined rental and leasing fleet of more than 800,000 vehicles. It is one of the biggest customers of General Motors, Ford, and several other car manufacturers. Indeed, Enterprise buys more new cars each year than any other company in the world. It's also the largest seller of used vehicles in the country, boasts the highest credit rating in its industry, and consistently ranks among the top twenty on *Forbes* magazine's annual survey of the largest private companies in America.

Even more impressive, Enterprise operates in an industry lit-
tered with countless failures and a reputation for low employee
morale, high turnover, bankruptcies, profit declines, and general
customer dissatisfaction. Despite this, the company has recorded
impressive gains each year for the past five decades. Enterprise
has never laid off employees, opens at least one new office every
business day, and has become *the* company to watch and emulate
when it comes to learning how to really wow your customers.

How has Enterprise done it? Above all, it adheres to an amaz-
ingly simply, yet ingeniously effective, philosophy set forth by
company founder Jack Taylor back on day one: "Take care of
your customers and employees, and the profits will follow."

Enterprise has an unbending determination to keep its customers happy—whatever it takes. At the same time, it strives to
hire the smartest and most talented people possible. Generally
speaking, nearly all employees at this family-owned company start
at the bottom and work their way up, even though a majority of
all new hires are college graduates. In fact, the company's quest
for bright, educated people has made it one of the largest
recruiters of newly minted graduates in the United States.

Following extensive formal and on-the-job training, Enterprise
gives its charges complete autonomy to run and grow their own
individual businesses, in turn creating opportunities for continuous advancement. What's more, very early in their management
careers, employees share in the company's profitability, meaning
the potential upside is theirs to realize. Individuals are empowered to act as entrepreneurs and are compensated accordingly.
People starting out behind the rental counter today can realisti-
cally work their way up to a six-figure salary over time by making smart business decisions and directing their own mini division
of the company. It's a structure that is almost unheard of in cor-

porate circles, yet it is directly responsible for fueling the company's astonishing growth. Indeed, it was a frontline employee who helped steer the company into the rental car business in the first place, and another who came up with the idea for its now defining "We'll Pick You Up" service.

What Enterprise knows is that in order for employees to provide outstanding customer service, they must be both committed to their jobs and properly incentivized. The two are very closely connected. Mere lip service or orders from on high won't cut it. That's why Enterprise has taken the unusual step of tying promotions—and therefore financial advancement—directly in to how well employees deliver on the company's promise to exceed customer expectations.

Keep in mind that at Enterprise, having "satisfied" customers isn't enough. The reason is straightforward and backed by research: When you *exceed* someone's expectations and bring them to the "completely satisfied" category, they are at least 70 percent more likely to do business with you again. And repeat business is the lifeblood of every company.

The strategy is clearly effective. Standard & Poor's calls Enterprise the most financially sound rental car company in the industry. In the last decade, workplace surveys conducted in four nations have included Enterprise among the best companies to work for, and its employees are often highly sought by recruiters at other firms—from a variety of industries. What's more, because of the company's unique focus on the fast-growing home-city, or off-airport, market segment, its business is nearly recession-proof.

Throughout this book, you'll go inside this amazing company and learn about "The Enterprise Way" of doing business. You'll discover how Enterprise has grown at such an impressive rate by outsmarting the competition, treating customers like royalty, and recruiting an army of top talent. More important, you'll learn tangible strategies you can use to stand out from the rest of the crowd, boost customer service, and attract key employees to your own business—regardless of what industry you're in.

We'll begin by looking at how Enterprise started and explore how this tireless pursuit to take care of customers and employees took hold. We'll also suggest strategies for ingraining such thinking into your own corporate culture. We'll then examine how Enterprise gained a competitive edge by following a different path than the rest of the rental car pack and by identifying markets that even the biggest players seemed to ignore.

Next, we'll reveal the company's strategies for hiring, training, and rewarding employees. Every Enterprise field employee starts as an entry-level management trainee, but the opportunities for career advancement are nearly unlimited. As you'll learn, Enterprise treats employees as entrepreneurs and compensates them as such. It's an unprecedented structure, more akin to having headquarters oversee a collection of nearly 7,000 independent locations.

The only way to move ahead at Enterprise is by delivering excellent customer service. To that end, we'll introduce you to the company's groundbreaking program for carefully measuring and monitoring how well each location is executing on this promise, and detail the importance these numbers hold for every aspect of the operation.

We'll then discuss how Enterprise has prospered by forming strategic partnerships with businesses of all types, while exploring how the company effectively uses technology to increase efficiencies and advance its business relationships.

We'll also talk about how Enterprise has been able to excel, even during a period of unprecedented growth, without jeopardizing customer service or employee morale. Much of it relates to the company's commitment to remain in "balance," as chairman and CEO Andy Taylor puts it, by staying equally focused on the following four core areas: growth, profitability, customer service, and employee development.

Finally, we'll look at the eight core values every Enterprise employee lives by. Because they tie directly back to founder Jack Taylor's vision, Enterprise calls them "Founding Values." They arguably can—and should—be adopted by companies of all types. These values include protecting your brand, creating a fun and friendly environment where teamwork rules, rewarding hard work, listening to your customers, strengthening the community, and always keeping your doors open to every person and every idea. Says company chairman and CEO Andy Taylor, "Founding values are the magnet that make all the shavings in your company point in the same direction." When you live by them, he insists, you become a special place and have an opportunity to distance yourself from the competition.

Does The Enterprise Way work for companies outside of the rental car industry? For an answer, you need look no further than Enterprise itself. The Taylor family also owns and operates a number of other diversified and completely unrelated businesses— from a distributor of in-room coffee packets to a manufacturer of Mylar balloons—all of which have enjoyed similar success by following these exact same techniques and management principles.

Thanks to its dedication to taking care of customers, and an impressive track record for profitability in the inherently low-margin rental car business, Enterprise is generally regarded as one of the world's best-run businesses by those who know the company well. Enterprise has also earned numerous outside awards, including a regular ranking at the very top of surveys on rental car companies conducted by J.D. Power and Associates.

At its heart, *Exceeding Customer Expectations* is your personal guide to running an employee-centered company catering to those who matter most—your customers.

You're about to learn how the Midwestern values and ingenuity Enterprise has so adeptly mastered can be applied to virtually any business to produce unbelievably satisfied customers, an entrepreneurial workforce committed to building the company, and record revenues.

Exceeding
Customer
Expectations

1

Take Care of Your Customers and Employees, and the Bottom Line Will Follow

TALL, IMPECCABLY DRESSED, silver-haired, and courtly, Enterprise Rent-A-Car founder Jack Taylor wears the mantle of corporate patriarch with surprising humility. His office is comfortable and well appointed, yet occupies space in an unassuming single-level building about two miles away from the company's modern five-story corporate campus in Clayton, a prosperous suburb of St. Louis, Missouri. The location of Jack's office has special significance, since it's the company's early headquarters and the exact same location he has worked in for decades—including the time he spent as CEO. Like the man himself, Jack's office holds fond memories of a career in the auto industry that began with anything but grand ambitions.

"I didn't start out wanting to get rich," he says when asked to explain the secret to his phenomenal success. "Making a huge amount of money was just not high on my list. Ensuring that customers were well taken care of and that employees were happy—those were the most important things. I figured if I did those two things well, I'd make money, because I would attract customers willing to pay a fair and decent price for what I was offering."

Fifty years after founding Enterprise on these very principles, the car rental behemoth has quietly become one of the most highly rated companies in the world based on multiple measures, including customer service, financial stability and growth, employee retention, and innovation.

While the notion of taking good care of your customers and employees is hardly new, the passion for delivering on this promise permeates every aspect of the company's operations. Enterprise doesn't just want its customers to be *satisfied*. The only way an employee can be promoted is by making sure customers are *totally satisfied* and convinced that Enterprise has done everything possible to exceed their expectations. As you'll learn, though virtually all Enterprise field employees start in entry-level management-trainee positions, it's possible for them to rise up the ranks and make impressive money—but only after demonstrating an ability to knock the socks off of every customer that comes through the door. That's because promotions are based on customer satisfaction, which the company continually tracks and monitors.

Although Jack Taylor remains involved in the company, son Andy has led Enterprise since 1980, first as president and now as chairman and chief executive officer. He's grown Enterprise far beyond what Jack himself admits he ever could have imagined. But Andy Taylor and the Enterprise team have accomplished this growth by rigorously following the bedrock principles first established by his father.

"The success of Enterprise is not based on technical proficiency or a complicated business model," Andy Taylor says. "We derive our success from careful adherence to a commonsense approach: We treat our customers well, we give our employees respect and opportunities to grow, and we know that if we stick to these two rules, profits and growth will naturally follow."

Make Everyone Feel Special

It goes without saying that all of us like to feel special and know that the people we are doing business with will go the extra mile for us. Enterprise's dedication to this is implicit in its famous slogan, "Pick Enterprise. We'll Pick You Up." The company will come get you at your house, or just about anywhere else, if you can't otherwise get to one of its branch offices to retrieve a loaner car. It's all part of the company's comprehensive customer service program.

One can recognize how serious Enterprise is about fulfilling this promise the moment you walk into a branch, or when an employee shows up to shuttle you to a waiting vehicle. They shake your hand, greet you by name, and look you in the eye while doing so. Enterprise employees don't suit up in uniforms bearing the company's trademark emerald green color. Instead, men wear button-down shirts and ties, and women don businesslike dresses or suits. Enterprise employees are professional yet friendly. They clearly enjoy what they're doing, and their enthusiasm and positive spirits are infectious. You can't help but feel good about doing business with these people, despite the circumstance that might have brought you in the door in the first place. And that's really the whole point.

Most Enterprise offices aren't very opulent. Many are housed in small spaces in unusual places, with only a handful of people working inside. But that is also part of the company's genius. Rather than fancy decorations, Enterprise offices are set up with convenience in mind. There's a branch within fifteen miles of 90 percent of the American population. The company also has a growing presence in Canada and Europe. Their point is that you're only going to be in the office for a short time—just long enough to get your car and go. Enterprise doesn't want you to have to stand in line. Instead, representatives find out when you want to pick up the car and set up the daily schedule in such a way that prevents too many customers from piling into the branch at once. In the event you have to wait, you'll likely be acknowledged by name and offered a cup of coffee. These are some of the basic niceties that turn first-time renters into longtime, loyal customers.

Enterprise's commitment to winning repeat business is what largely differentiates the company from the rest of the car rental industry. While most competitors are primarily concerned with getting renters in and out of cars as quickly as possible, Enterprise is singularly focused on making sure customers have a good experience and that they'll come back again. Repeat business has long been a key driver to the company's growth. Because many customers are referred to Enterprise either by an insurance company or some other business partner, the overall rental experience serves to shape each customer's opinion of the referring party as well.

Let's say you get in an accident and need to rent a replacement vehicle from Enterprise (which is highly likely, since most of the top auto insurers have preferred provider agreements with the company). You are already upset and frustrated when you walk into the Enterprise office, especially if the accident wasn't your fault. You don't want a *rental* car. You want *your own* car, which is likely in the shop for repairs and will never be quite the same again. If your experience with Enterprise is anything but excellent, you'll probably hold that against not only Enterprise, but also your insurance company, and maybe even the body shop and anyone else involved. On the other hand, if your dealings with Enterprise are pleasant, you'll have a favorable impression of both Enterprise and your insurance company.

Why is such repeat business so valuable? Because studies show it costs approximately five to six times more to gain a new customer than to keep a current one. If Enterprise is able to please customers during their first visit, even if they are originally introduced to the company under less-than-ideal circumstances, chances are they will come back the next time they need a car for a vacation or some other event.

WHY CUSTOMERS LEAVE

Over the years, Enterprise has learned that there are six primary reasons people will stop doing business with you:

- 1 percent die
- 3 percent move away
- 5 percent develop other relationships
- 9 percent leave for competitive reasons
- 14 percent are dissatisfied with the product
- 68 percent go elsewhere because of the poor way they were treated by employees of the company.

Successful retention, therefore, means building personal relationships with customers with the goal of keeping them for life.

Go Beyond the Call

Giving customers a lift is a crucial element of Enterprise's overall commitment to customer service. That commitment means going beyond sending a car for someone. It means doing whatever is necessary to take care of customers and satisfy their needs. In the eyes of Enterprise, customers are:

- The most important people that will ever walk into the office, either in person or otherwise.
- Not dependent on the company; instead, the company is dependent on them.
- Not an interruption of work, but the purpose of it.
- Not an outsider to the business, but a part of it.
- Not cold statistics—names on file cards or ledger sheets. They are flesh-and-blood human beings with biases, likes and dislikes, feelings, and emotions.
- Someone to satisfy, not argue with.
- People who bring their wants and needs into the office, which the company has a duty to profitably (and properly) fill.

If the employees handling your transaction at Enterprise seem more focused, engaged, and, yes, brighter than those you've met behind the counter at other rental car companies, that's because those are the kind of people Enterprise intentionally hires. Most are university graduates, a general prerequisite to gaining employment at the company. The reason? Enterprise isn't looking simply to hire counter clerks to check out cars. The company wants each employee to move up the leadership ladder. Some may one day become president or chief operating officer of the organization. (The current president and COO both started in entry-level management-trainee positions and worked their way up, as did CEO Andy Taylor.)

With few exceptions, field employees at the company, from the person behind the counter to executives at headquarters in St. Louis, begin as management trainees. The training program teaches employees how to run their own business. But their path to future advancement is based on each employee's ability to satisfy you, the customer. Not only has the company's "promote from within" policy helped to fuel growth and generate more revenue, it has opened countless new opportunities for the expanding workforce. Though profitability is a secondary consideration to the company, by operating under this "customers and employees first" philosophy, the bottom line continues to grow.

In fact, Enterprise has evolved into one of the most successful family-owned businesses in history. Its unique structure of giving entrepreneurial freedom and sharing profits with employees has created incredible worker loyalty, fostered innovation, and produced impressive financial results. What the company has learned over the years is that happy employees make for happy customers. That's why Enterprise spends so much time carefully choosing its people, training them properly, empowering them, and leading by example. It meticulously measures customer satisfaction, looks for ways to continually improve operations by using technology as efficiently as possible, and controls growth in such a way as to ensure that customer service is never compromised.

Customer Service Starts at the Top

To build a culture dedicated to customers and employees, it takes a real commitment from the top. The CEO must wholeheartedly believe in this concept in order to get everyone else on board and ingrain such thinking up and down the corporate ladder. Enterprise founder Jack Taylor was devoted to this notion long before going into business for himself, thanks to his traditional Midwestern upbringing.

Like many other members of "The Greatest Generation," by the time Jack entered the workforce, he'd already lived through a World War and the experience of combat. He felt lucky just to be alive. A Navy pilot in World War II, Jack flew combat missions in a Grumman F6F Hellcat off the decks of the USS Essex and USS Enterprise in the Pacific Theater. It was there, in the service, that he first discovered the importance of teamwork.

"In combat, they flew in pairs and utilized what was known as a Thatch weave," says Jack's son, Andy. "Basically, it was a defensive strategy where you looked out for each other. The military also gave my father a sense of mission and of getting things done as a team so you don't disappoint your teammates. In my mind, these things translated into business in the form of wanting to really make his customers like him, while creating a good and fun environment for those he worked with."

An indifferent student, Jack grew up feeling as if he was inferior to his classmates. "I despised Monday mornings more than anything as a kid, because I knew the teacher was going to call on me at school and I wouldn't get the answer right," he recalls. Upon graduating from high school in 1940, Jack enrolled in college, but only at his grandmother's insistence. After just one semester at Westminster College and another at Washington University, Jack dropped out of school to join the military after the attack on Pearl Harbor the following year. He went in with dreams of becoming a pilot.

"The Army rejected me because I had hay fever, so I tried the Navy, after learning it also had an air force," he says. "They told me I had to pass a test, which scared me because I did so poorly on tests in school. But for the first time I was motivated to do well. I was excited about the prospect of being a Navy pilot. I took the test and passed it through sheer determination."

Mastering his airplane, and being part of a team, gave Jack a sense of accomplishment he had never experienced before. He loved flying, and especially prided himself on making a perfect landing on the deck of the aircraft carrier every time.

"I felt like I was really in my element," Jack says. Cruising wingtip-to-wingtip in formation, the members of his "Air Group 15" focused on the same goals. Under the command of Captain David McCampbell, one of the Navy's all-time leading aces, their every movement was coordinated. "The beauty of teamwork is its simplicity," Jack says. "Everybody is in the right place, the leader points the way, and you all move together as one." The same thing, he later found out, is true in business.

Jack continued to fly combat missions as the war proceeded, serving as a wingman to many of the aces, including McCampbell, and seeing to it that pilots could execute attacks without being ambushed. When the USS Essex was sent back to port to refuel and rearm, he and several other junior pilots were assigned to fly combat missions from the USS Enterprise. "Enterprise" was a name that would later play an important role in his life.

By the time Jack left the service at the war's end in 1945, he had two Distinguished Flying Crosses and was newly married.

"Being in the military was one of the greatest experiences in my life. It really matured me," Jack says. "I went in a callow youth. By the time I left the service, I felt confident and believed I could accomplish whatever I set out to do."

Do the Right Thing

While the Navy taught Jack about teamwork and taking care of those around you, the concept of doing the right thing was instilled in him even earlier in life by his father, Melbourne "Mel" Taylor. A St. Louis stockbroker, Mel was a fun-loving and sociable man whose easygoing ways carried over into his business dealings. Mel was a man of integrity who taught Jack that who you are and how you act are more important than whether you make a lot of money.

"I remember one time Dad put together a business deal for a friend who was trying to expand his company," Jack says. "Because he trusted this guy, Dad didn't specifically discuss what would be in it for him, though he assumed he would be treated fairly. When the deal was done, I think Dad's friend sent him a case of whiskey. It was nice, but not much, given that Dad made the whole thing happen."

While Mel was disappointed, he didn't let it get him down. "Dad said to me, 'If that's how the guy wants to handle it, he's the loser, not me, because he lost his integrity,'" Jack recounts.

Now that Jack was back from the war, brimming with confidence and ready to start his new life as a married man, he sought guidance from his father.

"I asked Dad if the stockbrokerage business was a growing concern," he says.

In those days, the securities industry was a sleepy, leisurely paced business, as it had been since the 1929 crash chased much of the public away from the market. Mel told Jack that about six million shares were traded on the exchange each day. Maybe someday it would hit ten million.

"I wasn't impressed," Jack remembers. "It didn't look to me like the kind of fast-changing business with expanding opportunities that I was searching for."

Had Jack realized at the time that the securities industry would grow to handle billions of shares daily in around-the-clock trading, perhaps Charles Schwab would be competing against Enterprise Brokerage today. Instead, Jack decided to look elsewhere for other opportunities.

Following a short stint at the local newspaper, he bought a 1937 Chevrolet panel truck and started a local delivery service for businesses in the Clayton suburb of St. Louis. "I charged 25 cents a package and made deliveries to all kinds of customers, including runs for a drugstore," Jack recounts. "I convinced these small businesses that since the big department stores made deliveries, they needed to offer the service as well, and I was the guy to do it. I went in with plans to build the next UPS, which was still pretty small at the time." Jack worked long hours to expand his company, even enlisting his growing family's help. After his first child, Andy, was born in 1947, Jack often put him in a wicker basket, placed it on the passenger side of the truck, and brought Andy along on his evening delivery runs. Two years later, Jack had three more trucks and deliverymen, along with a new baby girl, Jo Ann.

Find Your Calling

The America Jack and his fellow soldiers came home to was about to go car crazy. Now that manufacturing facilities were no longer needed to build armaments, they could turn their attention to automobiles. Metal used for creating weapons could now be turned into fenders, door panels, hood ornaments, and big-block engines. And the demand for mobility far exceeded the available supply.

Among the beneficiaries of this trend was Arthur Lindburg, the father of one of Jack's childhood friends, Earl. He owned Lindburg Cadillac, a premier St. Louis dealership and distributor. Auto sales were in high gear as the postwar boom took hold, and Lindburg was looking for enthusiastic young men to join his business. He heard about Jack and had Earl call to ask whether he might want to work at the dealership. Jack said he was happy being his own boss and politely turned Earl down.

A few months later, Lindburg tried again, this time making the pitch in person. He was going out of town on a business trip, and asked Jack to accompany him on the drive to the airport. On the way, Lindburg got right to the point. He told Jack the car business was expanding and he wanted him to come work at the dealership. Jack explained that he knew nothing about the auto industry except for the bad reputation some dealers had because of the strong-arm tactics they used.

"What do you expect me to do at the dealership?" Jack asked.

"I don't know, we'll figure something out," Lindburg replied.

He then turned to Jack, looked him in the eye, and offered him $400 per month to take the job. That was 25 percent more than Jack made in his delivery business. While he enjoyed having his own company, Jack realized the opportunities for future growth would likely be much brighter at the car dealership. Besides, he was working seven days a week to keep the delivery business going, and with two children to feed, the boost in salary was hard to pass up. Before the end of the ride, Jack accepted Lindburg's offer.

"That," says Jack, "is how I got into the car business."

Challenge Established Practices

At twenty-six, Jack turned the delivery business over to one of his employees and went to work at Lindburg Cadillac. Rejecting the casual dress preferred by most car salesmen of the time, Jack wore a suit to work. The decorated combat vet was told to follow the porter around and make himself useful. Jack spent his first two weeks washing and prepping cars and sweeping floors. The menial labor didn't bother him, though.

"I never gave it a second thought," Jack says. "I just figured Lindburg would either use me in some valuable position or, if he didn't, I would leave and do something else."

After a few months, Jack became a used car salesman and

moved over to selling new vehicles shortly thereafter. He learned right away that Arthur Lindburg had a very different way of doing business compared to other car dealers at that time. Like his father, Lindburg was a man of high integrity who believed in treating customers right.

Given the high demand for automobiles, it was a seller's market, and dealers had numerous ways to squeeze extra profits out of every sale. "Automobile salesmen had a terrible reputation," Jack says. "I think a lot of people resented car dealers in general."

One reason had to do with a favored tactic of many dealerships known as the "T.O.," or "take-over." Two salesmen take on the role of "good cop, bad cop." The first negotiates with you and tries to get you to pay the highest possible price for the car. After going back and forth, the salesman comes up with a number that is clearly more than you are willing to pay. Declaring a stalemate, the first salesman responds, "Let me talk to my sales manager and see what I can do for you." At that point, the second, more personable, salesman takes over and negotiates a slightly lower price, but one that still has a nice profit built in for the dealership (despite what you might be told). By this time, your resistance starts to break. Largely out of exhaustion from all of the back-and-forth dealings, you agree to pay the dealer's price. Nevertheless, you probably leave feeling angry and cheated, with no intention of doing business at that dealership again.

Lindburg Cadillac became a respected business by eschewing such rough-elbowed tactics. Arthur Lindburg always told his salesmen to treat customers fairly, even if it meant making less money.

"A big challenge was keeping customers happy when their cars were delayed at the factory and not delivered on schedule," Jack recalls. "One day a hard-bargaining man offered me $400 to sell the first Cadillac that came in. Even though this was one month's pay, that car had been promised to someone else. While I gave up some nice money, it wasn't worth damaging my reputation over."

Lindburg abhorred many common industry practices. When Jack asked why he didn't use tactics like the generally accepted T.O. game, Lindburg replied: "I'll grant you that going along with this might allow us to make more money in the short term. But people aren't dumb. They can tell when you're trying to gouge them. So while you might increase profits in the short term, you'll eventually lose customers and wish you were doing business the right way, as we are now."

Jack developed a father-son relationship with Lindburg. Though Jack was thirty years younger, the two grew very close and talked about business like old friends. Despite Lindburg's commitment to taking care of customers, Jack felt there were some other areas in the dealership in need of improvement. For instance, when longtime loyal customers brought in their cars for service and required new windshield wiper blades, the dealership charged $5 for the labor to install them.

"We'd sell a guy a car and earn a $2,000 [in late-1940s dollars] profit and then make him angry by charging a petty amount to put on a windshield wiper blade that a filling station guy would do for free," Jack recounts. "I decided that when I finally had my own company someday, I would never do that. I wanted my customers to walk away thinking I ran a great place to do business. And I wanted the people who worked for me to come in saying, 'Hey, I like this place. Taylor's a good guy. He's honest, and he takes care of his customers.'"

Jack has carried this lesson into the practices of Enterprise today. While car rental customers generally don't need replacement wiper blades, employees find other ways to make transactions more pleasant without going after every nickel and dime. On hot days, for example, you may find an ice chest filled with cold drinks that are free for the taking. It costs the branch a few dollars, which indirectly comes out of the paychecks of those in management positions, given that they earn a percentage of overall profits. But they know it will create goodwill, leading to a better experience and the greater likelihood of a return visit in the future. This, in turn, translates into a better chance of promotions for them and higher profits for the company—yet another demonstration of how taking care of customers adds to the bottom line.

Think Ahead

After five years of selling Cadillacs, Jack was making good money—the equivalent of more than $250,000 a year in today's dollars. But as he contemplated his future, he began to recognize the limitations of being a car salesman. Jack realized the most he could probably hope for was eventually owning a dealership of his own. At the time, however, auto manufacturers only allowed individuals to own one location, thus limiting any upside potential. So Jack decided to turn his attention to a relatively new concept coming into the industry: automobile leasing.

Greyhound, the bus company, created a leasing division that was starting to attract the interest of some Cadillac customers in the St. Louis area. Knowing that another business was offering Cadillacs in his city infuriated Arthur Lindburg and got him thinking about starting a leasing division of his own. One of Lindburg's friends owned such a leasing company. When he came to town for a visit one weekend, Jack joined him for lunch to learn more about it.

Lindburg's friend explained how leasing worked and demonstrated the many financial benefits, especially for those wealthy customers who might otherwise buy outright. The more Jack heard, the more intrigued he grew. Not only did leasing sound like a good deal for customers, it also seemed to hold more potential promise than auto sales.

That night, as Jack reclined on his couch and stared at the ceiling, he wondered why someone would buy a car if he or she could lease one instead. Sure, purchasing outright still made sense for many, but leasing was a better option for some of the more well-heeled folks Jack worked with.

He was also intrigued by the potential benefits afforded to the owner of such a business. For starters, leasing companies didn't have to obtain a franchise from the manufacturer. They could open an office wherever they wanted, without geographic restriction, and had the freedom to lease any kind of car. If Chevrolet had a bad year with unpopular models, you could offer Fords or Oldsmobiles instead. You weren't required to carry an expensive inventory, because you only had to buy vehicles as leases were signed. Plus, there was no need for a service or parts department, since all of that was taken care of by the dealerships. As a result, you avoided the high costs associated with the overhead and infrastructure inherent in owning a dealership. On top of that, leasing was more flexible, enabling you to do a better job of meeting the unique needs of each customer. Jack especially loved that part of the business.

The following Monday, Jack went in to see Arthur Lindburg.

"Mr. Lindburg," he said. "You've been looking for someone to start the leasing business. I'd like to do it."

The two worked out a deal and agreed to form a partnership for this new venture. Lindburg bankrolled most of the up-front investment of $100,000. He decided there would be four equal partners: Lindburg and his two sons, Earl and Clinton, plus Jack.

After paying off his mortgage, Jack only had about $10,000 in cash on hand to contribute to his $25,000 in required equity. He planned to get a second mortgage for the rest, before Lindburg stepped in and loaned him the money.

There was just one problem. Although he was still shy of his thirtieth birthday, Jack had worked his way up to being general manager of the dealership and was earning a salary of $2,000 per month, plus sales commissions. Since no income was being generated from the leasing operation yet, Lindburg said he'd have to reduce Jack's monthly pay to just $750. While he understood the reasoning, Jack realized that wasn't enough to cover his bills. The two ultimately agreed on $1,000 a month plus bonuses, which would be reevaluated as the business grew.

"I remember my father coming home and saying, 'I'm going to take a pay cut at work,'" recalls Andy Taylor, who was just ten at the time. "Dad told us we had to take good care of our clothes, since they needed to last longer, and the Sunday-night steak and lamb chops were going out for a while."

Jack seemed to be about the only person around who thought it made sense to give up a cushy job at the city's premier dealership in exchange for a pay cut and a stake in a new business that had yet to prove itself. Even Jack's father tried to get him to reconsider. "'Do you know what you are doing, kid?'" Jack remembers him asking. "He thought I was crazy."

Make Good First Impressions

In February 1957, Jack started Executive Leasing (the precursor to what would become Enterprise). For the first year, Jack and his administrative assistant, Nell Mason, were the sole employees. The company operated from a basement office carved out of two car-service bays in the subterranean service department at Lind-burg's Clayton Cadillac dealership. Jack told everyone to refer to his office as being located on the "lower level" rather than "the basement," since it sounded much more impressive. First impressions, after all, were important to him.

In the early days, when a call came in, Jack would let it ring a few extra times so customers would think the office was busy. When auto mechanics on the other side of the plywood wall used their pneumatic tools, conversations came to a halt because of the loud noise.

At the time, few individuals understood the financial benefits of leasing over buying. But Jack knew if he could get the ear of potential customers at a certain income level and educate them about the merits of this alternative to ownership, he had a good chance of making a sale and beating out conventional car dealers. And because those who lease cars usually don't keep them as long as people who buy outright, that meant more potential repeat business. With Jack's commitment to taking care of customers, he knew they would be happy to come back when it was time for a new vehicle.

Slowly, the business began to grow.

"I remember Dad sitting at the kitchen table on Sundays working on rates for lease deals with a couple of pencils and graph paper," says daughter Jo Ann Taylor Kindle. "He had a map of St. Louis, and every time a customer would lease a car, he'd take a pin and put it on the map at the customer's street address. Andy and I would be down on our hands and knees watching him put these pins in the map. I remember he came home one day and said, 'I've got seven cars on the street.' He could tell you where every single car was in town."

Executive Leasing lost $30,000 its first year, broke even the second, and recorded a profit of $60,000 by year three. "It took ten years before we made our first million," Jack says. "Aside from year one, we have been a profitable entity ever since."

Surround Yourself with Like-Minded People

As the fledgling business grew and expanded into new areas, including car rentals, Jack looked for energetic, hardworking people to join the company. Most came through word of mouth, referred by mutual friends or relatives. Don Ross was courted after meeting one of Jack's first rental employees, Don Holtzman, at a party in 1964. Just out of his active-duty requirement with the National Guard, the twenty-one-year-old Ross seemed like a perfect candidate to join the operation. But Ross wasn't interested.

"I just bought a new car," Ross told Holtzman, "and every time I take it in for service, I feel like I'm getting ripped off." He ticked off a litany of complaints about dealerships in general and concluded, "I just don't think the car business is right for me."

Holtzman persisted. Hoping to put an end to the recruitment effort, Ross finally agreed to a one-on-one meeting with Jack Taylor.

"We've never met," Ross remembers Jack saying as he walked into his office, "but I absolutely understand your concerns about this business. In fact, before I had the opportunity to open up this company, I was a sales manager for the local Cadillac dealership, and I saw some of the things that you probably felt were distasteful or inappropriate."

This wasn't the kind of high-pressure sales pitch Ross expected.

"I made up my mind," Jack continued, "that if I ever had a chance to run my own business, the men and women who worked with me would always feel good about what they did, and they would promise to treat customers like family. I believe we've lived up to this. My goal is to find people willing to commit to those same ideals, and I hope you'll give the job your consideration. I really do believe you'll find we are different, and you can help to make us different. But it has to be your decision."

It was a hard pitch to turn down. "I thought I'd give it ninety days," Ross says. Now, forty-two years later, he is Enterprise's president and vice chairman in an organization with more than 62,000 employees.

True to Jack's word, the men and women who came to work for Enterprise have always been taken care of by the company and given the tools and support necessary to do the same for its customers. In turn, as Jack surmised, the bottom line has more than taken care of itself.

Foster Entrepreneurial Thinking

Opportunity is pure oxygen to those with an entrepreneurial spirit. A chance to try something new, put their skills to use, and create one great success after another. Providing such outlets for continual advancement is among the ways Enterprise takes care of its people.

Pam Nicholson is a tremendous example of this principle in action. An energetic, attractive blonde with an easy laugh, this St. Louis native was aware of Enterprise growing up but never thought much about working for the company. Then, after graduating from the University of Missouri in 1981, an employment agency suggested that she interview with Enterprise.

"I wanted a management-training position of some sort," she recalls, seated in her relaxed office at the corporate campus. "It was really the story they told me about the company and the opportunity that lay ahead that excited me. The performance-based pay and promotions were also appealing. This was the kind of environment I wanted."

Nicholson joined Enterprise as a management trainee. Within a year, she was an assistant branch manager. When her husband took a new job in southern California, she requested a transfer with Enterprise, which was in the early stages of its West Coast expansion. Over the next dozen years, Nicholson worked her way up to regional vice president of Orange County.

"My numbers were at the top of the charts in comparison to any of the branches, not only in California, but in the country," Nicholson says. "Regardless of where I was working, my goal was to make my branch, group, or area the very best, and no employee could give me any reason why we couldn't do it."

In recognition of the great numbers she put up, Enterprise brought Nicholson back to corporate headquarters as a corporate vice president in 1994, where she oversaw the efforts of ten different operating groups. She also helped to establish the first national preferred-provider rental agreements between Enterprise and many top auto manufacturers. In 1996, Nicholson was promoted to general manager of the New York group. While it was the company's second largest, it was an operation that still had great potential for significant growth.

"There were a lot of tough challenges to doing business in New York," Nicholson says. "Some said we couldn't have a profit there because property prices were so high, too many cars got stolen, and it was hard to find good people." Nicholson's answer: "Let's talk about how we can overcome these challenges one at a time, because with challenges come great opportunities."

Nicholson and her team transformed those opportunities into successes and turned the New York group into one of the company's most profitable. Today, in her mid-forties, she is back at headquarters as Enterprise's chief operating officer and the third-highest-ranking officer in the company. We'll look at the methods she and other top performers have used to achieve such impressive results in coming chapters.

Stand Tall in Tough Times

The real test of what a company is made of, and its commitment to employees and customers, often comes during times of crisis. Enterprise had a chance to demonstrate how it responds in such situations more than once in recent years.

One opportunity came on September 11, 2001. The terrorist attacks in New York, Washington, and Pennsylvania that morning stranded hundreds of thousands of travelers across the United States. As the air transportation system shut down, Enterprise branches filled up with travelers looking for a way to get home to destinations hundreds, and sometimes thousands, of miles away.

Because of the decentralized nature of its business, combined with relatively low customer interest, Enterprise doesn't offer one-way or drop-off rentals. But as the dimensions of the calamity became apparent, managers independently decided to let stranded customers take the cars wherever they needed to go. Headquarters quickly signed on to the plan. They determined that getting people home was the most important thing. To facilitate this process, branch managers organized customers by destination, filling cars with strangers who were all going in the same direction, given the limited supply of vehicles. Up to 5,000 cars were displaced as a result. It took months to get all the cars back where they came from or to sell them off the lots where they ended up. But Enterprise never hesitated, in spite of the cost.

"All of the other rent-a-car companies near Dulles Airport closed down and put buses out in front blocking the entrance so customers couldn't get in," Ross remembers. "They were sold out and just turning people away. By contrast, one of our managers discovered there were several hundred people in his lobby looking for a car. He and his team came out and assured the crowd they'd do whatever they could to take care of them."

First, the manager opened up the soda and snack machines, and told everyone to help themselves. He then set up two phones and allowed people to call their loved ones free of charge, to let them know where they were and that they were making arrangements to rent a car and get home.

"Organizing these car pools of people going to the same location was the solution we came up with to take care of everyone, given the limited supply of available cars," Ross explains. "Again, the other rental car companies got word from corporate to close down. We decided to take care of our customers, despite the costs and systemic challenges of dealing with all these displaced cars."

Enterprise was forced to act again after Hurricane Katrina hit in 2005, devastating much of the Gulf region. After quickly setting up a process to ensure the safety and whereabouts of all employees in the affected areas, the company's next priority was making sure representatives from the Federal Emergency Management Agency, Red Cross, and the insurance company catastrophe teams had vehicles, since they were the frontline help in getting dislocated lives back in order. It was only after addressing the most crucial needs during that chaotic time that Enterprise turned its attention to locating the hundreds of dislocated cars, including those that were completely destroyed by the hurricane and subsequent flooding.

Some rental companies with cars available following the disaster raised daily fees to astronomical levels, given the huge demand. The same thing happens in local areas during major events, such as the Super Bowl. "We don't price-gouge," Ross insists. "The main reason is this: If you need a car during one of these times and we charge you $120 for a car that's normally $40, even though you're happy to have the vehicle, you don't feel good about what you're being charged. The next time you need to rent a car, we want you to think about us, instead of remembering that we took advantage of you. It's all about long-term thinking instead of focusing on short-term gains."

As for taking care of its people, what employee wouldn't relish being able to help people out in such a meaningful way, knowing that he or she had the authority to make this decision, and feeling reassured that the company would back them up because they were doing the right thing? That's a big part of what taking care of both your employees and your customers is all about.

THE ENTERPRISE WAY

1. Concentrate foremost on taking the best possible care of your employees and customers. Profitability will naturally follow.
2. Don't just endeavor to make customers *satisfied*. Treat them so well they'll be *totally satisfied*.
3. Rather than fancy decorations, set up your place of business with customer convenience in mind.
4. It's the basic niceties—shaking hands and greeting people by name—that turn first-time renters (or shoppers or clients) into lifetime loyal customers.
5. Repeat business is crucial, because it costs between five

and six times more to gain new customers than to keep current ones.

6. View your customers as the most important people who will ever walk through your doors.

7. A total commitment to customer service must begin at the highest level of the organization.

8. Never compromise your integrity.

9. Abhor practices that are unfair to your customers, even if they are considered commonplace in your industry. While crossing the line might increase profits in the short term, such actions will prevent people from wanting to do business with you again.

10. Avoid charging customers for small services that cost you little or nothing to perform, especially with customers who do business with you on a regular basis.

11. Uncover opportunities that will serve you well over the long haul.

12. Go the extra mile to make good first impressions.

13. Surround your business with like-minded, entrepreneurial people and listen to what they have to say.

14. Be ready to act and stand tall in times of crisis, even if it means taking a temporary hit to the bottom line in order to do what is right.

To Gain a Competitive Edge, Be Different

UNCOMMON SUCCESS COMES with uncommon approaches to business. In a crowded field, you must make your business stand out. This doesn't mean simply erecting fancy signs or engaging in promotional gimmickry. The fundamentals of the product or service you offer must be genuinely unique. Just *looking* different from the competition isn't good enough. The difference has to give you a quantifiable competitive advantage.

For instance, in addition to low fares, Southwest Airlines has long distinguished itself by its joke-cracking flight attendants, who help to forge a personal bond between the airline and its passengers in what is otherwise a commodity business. By the same token, FedEx made reliability and the ability to instantly track a package through every step of the delivery process a major point of differentiation among other overnight shipping alternatives.

Likewise, Enterprise has always tried to be very different from everyone else in the car rental business. This desire to buck conventional wisdom is something Jack Taylor has prided himself in from the very beginning. And it allowed the company to take ownership of what has since become the largest and most profitable segment of the car rental industry.

Stand Out from the Crowd

When it comes to renting a car, Hertz, Avis, Budget, National, Alamo, Thrifty, Dollar, and Enterprise all pretty much offer the same mix of makes and models. In the highly competitive rental car industry, the cost of a daily rental tends to be fairly similar, especially among like providers, and the transaction process is about the same across the board. So why do customers continually choose Enterprise and place it at the top of the heap? Quite simply, even in what is often described as a commodity-driven business, Enterprise has found many ways to truly stand out in a very crowded field.

While the most obvious difference is Enterprise's attention to service, the company also sets its products apart in other ways— the location of its branches, the professional appearance and friendly attitude of its employees, and most famously, the door-to-door service touted in its trademarked slogan, "Pick Enterprise. We'll Pick You Up."

Behind the scenes, Enterprise is fundamentally dissimilar from its major competitors as well. Its rental operation began by serving non-airport customers, a completely different segment of the rental market. It has a unique management and organizational structure, along with an unprecedented compensation system. Its people are educated, career-oriented, and thrive on being part of a team-oriented entrepreneurial environment. Enterprise is also a privately held, family-owned company, which means it isn't subject to the same pressures for quick returns and pumped-up profits that much of its major competition faces. As a result, the company can devote its resources to doing what's best for everyone over the long term.

Make no mistake, the rental car business isn't rocket science. As the folks at Enterprise will readily admit, in some ways the company's meteoric rise is a testament to the KISS adage—keep it simple, stupid. The company's core operating principles are built on the bedrock business values first laid out by Jack Taylor and now carried on by his son, Andy. But some of Enterprise's greatest successes have come about largely because, from the very beginning, Jack always put his own unique touch on things—even if it meant bucking industry standards and the advice of those around him.

Dress for Success

Jack Taylor's desire to be different first came about in reaction to the disappointing practices he saw within the auto industry. He abhorred the strong-arm tactics used by many other car dealers and wanted to treat his people right. While fellow salesmen dressed in loud casual wear, Jack made sure his people always presented a professional appearance, closer to that of bankers.

As research later revealed, professionally dressed employees put the customer at ease. By the same token, a professional look helps Enterprise employees present a business-savvy appearance, while showing respect and exuding confidence when servicing customers of all ages. In many operating groups, the company even gives new recruits a special allowance to help pay for nicer clothes.

"I've had customers tell me, 'When I walk up to the counter of one of your places, the people always look nice,'" Jack says. "It shows customers we are a serious, respectful business that is going to treat them well."

That said, you must also ensure your dress code is in line with local customs. That's a lesson Enterprise learned the hard way. When the company first moved into south Florida, the three-piece suits worn by some of its employees seemed to be a stumbling block to building business in an area known for its more casual dress style. Once suits were replaced by slacks, light-colored jackets, and ties, business took off. In the laid-back state of Hawaii, Enterprise finally gave up on ties altogether and embraced the ubiquitous Aloha shirt as standard business attire (although Enterprise's Hawaiian shirts have button-down collars), after encountering similar reactions to the more formalized appearance.

"When we first moved into Hawaii, some on the islanders came up to our people and said, 'Are you guys with the IRS?' since they were walking around in their white shirts and ties," Andy Taylor recalls. "We quickly realized that type of dress wasn't going to work there."

Company leaders took a lot of flak for their professional dress requirement when other major corporations adopted a "corporate casual" policy during the 1990s at the height of the dot-com boom. There was even discussion about at least instituting casual Fridays at Enterprise. But Jack didn't think it was right for the company.

"I remember one of our managers said to me, 'If we go the casual route, the first day will be our best-dressed day and it will go downhill from there,'" he says.

In the years since, companies have found that casual dress, in part, leads to a loss of focus and can result in declining profitability, which was Jack's belief all along. Studies show there is a direct correlation between how one dresses, thinks, acts, feels, and behaves. There's also a link to how others respond and react to those with a nice appearance. Given this, the trend away from dressing up is now starting to reverse itself.

"The bottom line is that people act the way they look," Jack says. "Nice dress gives you a much higher degree of authority and commands the respect of your customers."

Many Enterprise employees say they prefer dressing professionally because it increases their self-esteem and makes clients more respectful. Jack also feels it's crucial for Enterprise employees to *speak* as professionally as they *dress*.

"This is something I picked up early on," Jack explains. "The automobile industry used to have a lot of slang expressions. People would say, 'We're going to get you a car with the heat and the music and deep tread on the tires.' I said, 'Don't talk automobile talk. Don't sound like a car jockey. Speak like a banker.' A solid vocabulary gives you credibility, and people, in turn, feel more comfortable doing business with you."

Go Your Own Way

By 1961, Executive Leasing boasted three St. Louis locations: the original basement—or lower level—at Lindburg Cadillac in Clayton, a branch on South Kingshighway, and one downtown on Market Street. The company now had more than 1,000 of its cars on the street, with a customer base that had grown beyond the upscale trade Jack first cultivated to include an ever-diverse group of those from the middle class.

Doug Brown and Don Ross, both in their early twenties, were selected to run the downtown office. The two worked hard making sales calls and following up on leads, but business got off to a quiet start. Brown knew the Cadillac salesmen next door didn't think they were working very hard, so he and Ross went the extra mile to keep up appearances.

"Anytime you're going somewhere," Brown told Ross, "carry a clipboard and walk fast so it looks like you're in the middle of doing something."

As the leasing business picked up, the company discovered yet another differentiating service that would prove to be the most significant one of all: car rentals.

All Roads Lead to Rentals

The automobile rental business was born early in the last century. Legend has it that Joe Saunders of Omaha, Nebraska, conducted the first rental transaction in 1916, after rigging a mileage meter on his secondhand Model T Ford and offering it out for anyone to drive at the rate of ten cents a mile. His first customer was reportedly a traveling salesman who rented the car for a date with a local girl. By the mid-1920s, Saunders's rental company operated in twenty-one states, though it went bankrupt during the Depression.

The oldest surviving company (though it has changed hands numerous times) started in 1918, when Walter L. Jacobs opened a car rental business in Chicago with a fleet of about a dozen Model Ts. By 1923, the company was grossing $1 million in annual sales. Jon Hertz acquired the business through his Yellow Cab and Yellow Truck and Coach Manufacturing Company, and it later became known as the Hertz Drive-Ur-Self System, now Hertz Rent-A-Car.

With railroads the primary means of long-distance travel, some early car rental companies established branches in railway stations. The real explosion in business came with the expansion of airline travel in the postwar period. When jet aircraft entered the civilian fleet, the buses and trains that previously formed the backbone of the national public transportation network withered as travelers sought their own rental vehicles to get them around town in faraway places.

By the 1960s, a few national companies dominated the car rental industry, and almost all had offices located exclusively at airports. By the middle of the decade, more than 135,000 rental cars were on the road in the United States, and the industry posted revenues of $450 million. The cost of competing with the handful of established operators was high. In fact, the Federal Trade Commission sued Hertz, Avis, and National for monopoly practices in 1975, alleging that they conspired to keep new competitors from entering the market. (The case was settled out of court.)

Jack Taylor viewed the rental car business as a cutthroat, crowded industry with a questionable future. To him, leasing initially seemed to be a far more attractive option. But the great thing about opportunity is that, like beauty, it is in the eye of the beholder. Opportunities are always in our midst. Sometimes they fall into our laps dressed as problems or unwanted distractions. That's why one should constantly be on the lookout for opportunity in its many forms, and encourage this same kind of thinking from everyone in the organization.

At times, opportunity comes looking for you. In order to recognize it underneath whatever disguise it may be wearing, you must push back the boundaries of what you consider an opportunity to be, as the huge trajectory of Enterprise's growth and success underscores.

Be Open to Opportunity

Lindburg Cadillac had long maintained loaners for customers with cars in the shop for servicing or repairs. There were half a dozen Chevrolets and a Cadillac in the loaner fleet—when they could be found.

At the same time, some of Jack's leasing customers would occasionally come in looking for loaners when relatives were visiting from out of town, or when the vehicles they leased were in for service. But as much as he believed in superior customer service, renting cars was one of his customers' needs that Jack wanted no part in fulfilling. Arranging the rental was too time-consuming for his salespeople, and it took them away from their core leasing clientele.

"We started out saying, 'We don't rent cars,'" Jack recalls.

But Jack's customers weren't accustomed to hearing "No."

"Good customers would get kind of mad," Jack says. "So we'd reluctantly tell them, 'Okay, we'll give you something for these short-term needs.'" Sometimes he'd even borrow a car or two from Lindburg's loaner fleet.

Arthur Lindburg didn't like dealing with loaner cars, or the rental business, either. He decided that Executive Leasing should buy the dealership's loaner fleet and rent the cars back to him as needed. Jack dutifully agreed. But even though he wasn't very interested in the rental business, Jack realized he had to run the rental operation with the same high standards as the leasing business. His reputation was on the line, after all. A fleet of junkers wouldn't do, and just making this a part-time venture wasn't in anyone's best interest.

"One day I decided we either had to stop renting cars or we had to go into the car rental business," Jack says. He wound up choosing the latter option.

One Friday afternoon in 1963, Jack approached Don Holtzman.

"I said to Don, 'It's a big pain doing these one-off rentals,'" Jack remembers. He then asked whether Holtzman would like to run a rental car company if he set one up. Holtzman eagerly agreed.

"Come in Monday and tell me how many cars you want and we'll be in the rental business," Jack told him.

Monday morning, Holtzman informed Jack that he needed seventeen cars. No one knows how Holtzman came up with the number. "Nevertheless, I said, 'Okay,'" Jack says with a chuckle, "and we bought seventeen cars."

The fleet consisted of two-door and four-door Chevrolets. The rental rate was set at $5 per day and 5 cents per mile. Given that the customer base would come largely from existing Lindburg Cadillac and Executive Leasing clients, no one expected much from the new sideline. To drum up extra business, Holtzman and his team posted flyers in nearby office buildings and sent mailings about the rental car service to local businesses. But it was designed strictly as an adjunct to the company's primary auto-leasing business.

Keep Knocking on Doors

Doug Brown and Don Ross had a fleet of ten rental cars (one Corvair and nine Impalas) at the downtown branch they were tasked to run. As they struggled to drum up business for the new office, they were struck by a bit of inspiration.

Walking back from lunch one day, Brown and Ross passed by a building that housed the insurance arm of AAA Missouri. Ross suggested they stop in to talk with the insurance adjuster. At the time, insurance companies offered policyholders money for either cab fare or to pay for a car rental in the event their vehicle was stolen or damaged in an accident. Maybe, Brown reasoned, the adjuster would rather offer customers the rental car itself instead of just handing out money, especially if the insurance company could better control its expenses. The adjuster eagerly listened to their pitch: "$5 a day, 5 cents per mile." While the $5 a day was okay, the adjuster explained that his company didn't want to pay mileage charges, which could quickly add up. Brown and Ross agreed to give up the mileage fee in exchange for billing the insurance company directly for the rental. The adjuster agreed to give it a try.

Without realizing it at the time, Brown and Ross had just made their first sale to a vast, untapped pool of potential renters, a market segment that would eventually drive Enterprise to become the largest car rental company in North America. It's what is now referred to as the "home-city" market—renting to local residents who need temporary transportation due to an accident, repair, out-of-town guests, or the need for a different car to accommodate any variety of needs. And it began a partnership that would fuel unprecedented new opportunities.

"Nobody even knew that the off-airport market existed then," Jack says.

A short time later, their first insurance customer arrived at the office. Grizzled and scruffy, the man wore a T-shirt with a pack of Lucky Strikes rolled into his sleeve. Both wondered if this was Jack's idea of the kind of customer they should be dealing with in the normal leasing trade.

Whereas Jack gave his employees plenty of autonomy, he left no doubt about what he expected of them. Jack and his staff held periodic meetings to discuss every bad lease they had written, in an effort to uncover clues that could help them avoid getting hooked up with a similarly risky prospect in the future. In those meetings, Jack often advised his team, "Don't lease a car to someone you wouldn't lend your own car to."

As their first rental customer left with the keys, Ross shook his head. "That's not our kind of customer. If you wouldn't rent him your own car, don't rent him one of mine," he said, echoing Jack. "I'm getting out of this business."

"You're wrong," Brown quickly corrected him. "I'd rent him my car. We know he has insurance since he's one of their customers, and we know he's good for the bill since we're being paid directly by the Auto Club."

As the number of insurance customers began to increase, the rental team (consisting of Don Ross, Wayne Kaufman, and Don Holtzman) talked briefly with Jack about their plan to approach other insurers looking for customers. Jack saw the potential but didn't know if there was really enough business out there to justify diverting resources from the leasing side of the company.

"All right," Jack decided after considering their proposal. "I'm going to let you go with this. But I reserve the right to say 'I told you so' if it doesn't work out."

Just as Jack wouldn't operate with a fleet of beat-up cars, he refused to conduct his rental business with anything less than the same kind of service enjoyed by his leasing company clients. When insurance companies called Executive (which would later come to be known as Enterprise) to arrange for a rental after being notified about an accident by a policyholder, the company had all of the paperwork filled out in advance and greeted customers by name and with a handshake.

Before long, MIC (Motors Insurance Corporation), a division of General Motors that had an office across the street from Executive's downtown location, also signed on to the rental car replacement plan. The rental operation began to build as the three-man rental team hit the streets to drum up business. Through diligence and determination, they had unwittingly created yet another key differentiator that set the company apart from the competition.

Uncover New Markets

Operating in the home-city market was clearly unique and unconventional, but it offered several important advantages: It reduced competition, because almost every other rental car company was located at the airport, targeting business travelers. It made the cost of entry and doing business cheaper, since operating expenses were much lower in town. The home-city market also allowed the company to stress its primary differentiator—customer service. That's especially crucial when dealing with those who have been in an accident, as is true of many of the company's insurance-referral renters.

"These customers were disoriented and upset because everything had gone wrong," says Jack, describing what it was like to receive these customers in the early days. "The tow truck driver might have been short-tempered, the people at the service station probably only had bad news, and now they came to some rental car company they'd never heard of, thinking, 'Okay, what are *these* people going to do to me?'"

What happened, more often than not, was that Jack's people acted as grief counselors. They expressed compassion, reassuring customers that accidents happen to the best of drivers, and that as long as they were okay, an accident really wasn't a big deal in the greater scheme of things. Meanwhile, employees handled all the paperwork and explained that the customer didn't have to pay anything, since it was all being taken care of by the insurance company. Probably for the first time since hearing that awful sound of scraping metal, customers could finally start to rebuild their lives and begin to relax.

Jack pursued a go-slow policy in expanding the rental business, as he did with leasing. But the company's greatest differentiator was still to come. And, like the home-city market, it's a concept that arose from the perseverance and ingenuity of its people.

Be Open to Change

By 1971, Executive had five offices in St. Louis. The largest branch had a rental fleet of 85 cars. (Today the fleet size at a typical home-city location is about 110 cars. If a branch needs more than that, the company opens a new location nearby to handle the overflow, which then gives a group of employees the chance to build their own new business from scratch.) The company also had a branch in Atlanta—strictly a leasing operation—that opened in 1969. This was about the time the company changed its name from Executive to Enterprise. As it moved to new areas, the company found itself competing with other "Executive Leasing" businesses, since the name was so generic. Because Jack wanted to keep the trademark "e" logo, he knew any new name had to start with that letter. "Essex" (in honor of Jack's Navy ship the USS Essex) was among the names proposed, but "Enterprise" (the other ship he served on) won out. Not only did Enterprise have considerable sentimental value, it also seemed more prestigious than the other options on the table. "Essex sounded kind of stodgy," Jack says.

Despite his initial reluctance, Jack felt the rental business model—which continued to be built on developing relationships with insurance companies, body shops, and car dealers—was working well. He decided to expand this concept even further. Jack and his team began looking for the next location to move into. They wanted a midsized city in the Southeast that showed moderate to strong growth. In the end, they settled on Orlando, Florida. Walt Disney World had just opened, and the prospects for market growth looked promising. Moreover, the auto insurance business in Florida was about to undergo a monumental change that would help both drivers and Enterprise: the enactment of "no-fault" insurance.

The no-fault concept gained acceptance in the early 1970s as part of a reform movement that also saw the breakup of telephone monopolies and regulated airlines. Previously, drivers involved in an accident had to wait until it was determined exactly who was at fault before insurance companies would pay out money for a car rental or anything else. Under no-fault laws, adopted by a score of states, each insurance company was responsible for paying the claims of its insured immediately after being filed.

Jack wanted to make sure his Orlando office, as the company's first pure rental location outside of St. Louis, was a success. He asked one of his best leasing managers, Bob Bell, to open it. Jack then tapped Lanny Dacus, who had joined the company less than a year before, as Bell's assistant.

Dacus had an ice cream shop across the street from Enterprise's second office on South Kingshighway on the south side of St. Louis. After Dacus lost his lease and closed the shop, he took a sales job with a pharmaceutical company, but soon left because he didn't agree with its ethics. He'd always been impressed with the Enterprise people, so he went to Ross looking for a job. At age thirty, Dacus was almost an old man compared to some of the other members of the team. They wondered whether he could keep up with Enterprise's frenetic pace. To show them he could, Dacus offered to work free for six months to prove himself. The company decided to hire him—with pay—because of his enthusiasm alone, and he was sent to work at the newly opened West Florissant Road office in Dellwood, Missouri.

Since insurance companies, which were closed on the weekends, made up almost all of Enterprise's rental customers, whatever rental cars were on the lot on Friday afternoon stayed there until Monday morning. Though he was still new to the job, Dacus didn't like the thought of these vehicles sitting around idle, so he tried to figure out a way to turn them into revenue generators during this off-peak time.

Inspiration hit one day when an employee of the New York City Transit Authority (NYCTA) stopped by the Kingshighway office. The St. Louis Car Company, one of the city's leading businesses, made subway cars for the NYCTA. Every two or three weeks, a small group of Transit Authority employees came through town for an orientation about the newest subway cars. The NYCTA kept a loaner vehicle in St. Louis for its people to use when they were in the area. During one trip, the car was stolen, and the transit worker turned to Enterprise for a replacement.

As Dacus filled out the paperwork, he asked, "What do you do when you're in town?"

The man confessed that his days were spent in class and he had little to do on the weekend, since he didn't know anyone in town and had to share the same car with his colleagues.

"I'll tell you what," Dacus offered. "What if I pick you up on Friday, show you some places to drive to around here over the weekend, and let you bring the car back in on Monday?"

"We would all love that," the man replied.

Thus began a whole new business venture for the company: weekend leisure rentals. Instead of sitting idle in the parking lot, Enterprise vehicles could now be making money on both Saturday and Sunday, even while the office was closed.

In addition to picking them up, Dacus created a package for weekend clientele containing a map of the area showing various points of interest. He also included brochures for all major attractions in the region.

"Customers loved it, and it was really boosting revenue," Dacus says. "And because these counted as leisure rentals, we could charge for mileage, which sometimes really added up when they decided to hit all the spots on the map."

In his spare time, Dacus helped sell used cars for Lindburg, "just for something to do." He soon became the second-highest volume salesman on the lot. Word of what Dacus was doing made it back to the main office. It prompted Jack Taylor to pay a visit to the location.

Jack walked up to Dacus and said, "Sport, tell me what you're doing."

At first, Dacus thought he was in trouble.

"I know I'm not supposed to be picking people up," Dacus responded, explaining the weekend program he'd put together and showing Jack one of the packages with the map and brochures. He also gave Jack a written script he had developed to help sell cars.

"Can I have a copy of that?" Jack asked.

They chatted a little more. As Jack was about to leave, he looked Dacus in the eye and said, "This pick-up and delivery—just watch what you're doing."

That was the last Dacus heard from Jack until he got the call about going with Bell to Orlando.

Pick Customers Up

Bell and Dacus began scouting locations for the new office while making sales calls on insurance companies, claims adjusters, and auto dealers. They spread the word about Enterprise and what the company could do for these businesses, hoping to replicate the model that had worked so well in the Midwest.

Car theft accounted for a significant portion of the insurance replacement rental market. It presented a unique challenge for Enterprise. Policies typically allowed insurance companies to wait forty-eight hours before paying for a replacement rental vehicle, enough time to see whether the stolen car could quickly be recovered. But customers needed cars right away. Rather than lose out on this business, Dacus came up with a solution: If the insurance company would pay for the rental right away, he would take two days off the rental bill if the car was found within this forty-eight-hour period. Not only would this bring in business to Enterprise that would otherwise be lost, it would turn the insurance company into a star in the eyes of its customers. Everyone won—the customers most of all. Insurers could tell policyholders, "While we technically don't have to provide a car for you until the day after tomorrow, we'll start the rental right away because we want to get you back on the road as quickly as possible." And as it turned out, Enterprise rarely had to absorb a charge for a car found within forty-eight hours, since so few stolen cars were recovered that fast.

"We considered it to be a very calculated risk," Jack says.

No-fault insurance took effect in Florida in January of 1972, and business at the Enterprise branch on East Colonial Drive in Orlando began to grow. Bell and Dacus told Jack they planned to have fifty cars in the rental fleet by Christmas. Though they fell a couple short of that, considering that the largest rental fleet at any existing branch was eighty-five cars, it was a big number for such a new office.

As the benefits of no-fault insurance became clear to consumers, small accidents that would have otherwise gone unreported before were now being filed. Insurance companies couldn't keep up with claims; body shops were inundated with work. "All of a sudden, we went from 50 to 75 to 80 cars, and business began to explode," Dacus recalls.

Dacus printed up cards with a map on the back showing insurance customers how to get to the Enterprise office. But, given that most customers had no car, they still had trouble finding their way to the branch. In most cases, their vehicle was incapacitated and towed directly to a body shop. Frustrated body shop managers and dealerships started calling Dacus, asking him to please come pick these people up.

"I'd say, 'Yes,'" Dacus recalls. He was willing to do what it took to get the business, even though providing such transportation wasn't part of company protocol. Before long, shuttling customers became more and more common.

Enterprise placed its branches in parts of town where car dealerships and repair shops were concentrated, so customers were never that far way. But Dacus realized this new shuttle service could also help out with another problem. With business surging, the office got so crowded at peak times that lines grew long and transactions backed up. Making customers wait wasn't the kind of customer experience Bell and Dacus wanted to deliver.

To solve this dilemma, when renters or an insurance company called to reserve a car, Dacus found out when they planned to show up for it. If it was at a peak time, he would offer to come pick the customer up at their home or office—but at a time when things would likely be a bit calmer at the branch. This helped to prevent customer overload and allowed Enterprise to earn a reputation for great customer service around town. It was known as the car rental company that picked customers up.

When word of what Dacus was doing got back to headquarters, Doug Brown was assigned to follow up on Dacus's latest innovation.

"'Lanny,' I said, 'we are a cash-and-carry business, and that means you carry it away,'" Brown recalls. "'People need to find their own way in here. Free delivery? Are you crazy? If you offer that, they won't go out of their way to even try to come in themselves. You'll be sorry.'"

But Dacus was convinced the service would attract even more business for the company.

"Go ahead and do it," Brown said, echoing the words of Jack Taylor. "But I reserve the right to tell you I told you so."

By that spring, inventory at the Orlando branch skyrocketed to 175 cars, more than any other Enterprise location. It was also highly profitable. Jack called in every Friday to check the numbers and see how business was progressing.

"I understand you're doing a little pick-up and delivery," Jack said to Dacus during one of his weekly calls. Dacus admitted it was true and filled Jack in on the hows and whys. Jack listened intently.

"Lanny," he said, "I want to underpromise and overdeliver. I don't want you to offer anything we can't provide when we get bigger. Whatever you start today, we have to continue."

Jack didn't tell Dacus to stop, though, and this unusual pick-up plan soon spread to other Enterprise offices. "Has Lanny lost his mind?" some managers wondered when told about the initiative. But after seeing the overwhelmingly positive results, more offices gradually began to embrace this pick-up service as well. They came to realize it was an important differentiator between Enterprise and its competitors, since nobody else offered anything similar. It instantly gave Enterprise an advantage in the marketplace.

Promote What Makes You Different

By the time the company launched its first national advertising campaign in the late 1980s, providing pick-up service for customers was common companywide policy. The idea of building a television commercial around this concept really took hold in 1988, as Jack Taylor got dressed one morning. He couldn't help but notice the plethora of automobile commercials airing on the TV playing in the background. It struck Jack that, while Enterprise pioneered the concept of offering great customer service in the home-city car rental industry, few outside of the company knew this. What if one of his competitors beat him to the game with an ad claiming *they* were the experts in home-city rental and the first to come up with the idea? How would he feel if a commercial for another rental car company appeared on TV promoting the fact that Enterprise's competition would come get you at your home, repair shop, or business? In short order, Jack decided that Enterprise must act quickly in order to secure this unique piece of real estate in the minds of consumers.

Jack discussed the task of creating a national ad campaign with Andy, who wanted to make sure the process was appropriately managed to contain costs and keep top managers engaged. Enterprise began by forming an advertising committee, led by Jack and Andy. It included top-level managers and officers from around the country. Since the company was experiencing strong growth and local advertising efforts seemed to be effective, many in the organization were less than enthusiastic about creating a national campaign, especially given that the cost would come out of their profits. In fact, a majority of people expressed serious concerns about the idea.

In one of those rare instances when a decision by local leadership was overridden by corporate, Jack told them, "I outvote you all." He then determined that, despite their hesitancies, plans for a companywide ad campaign would proceed. This was the only time managers could recall Jack pulling rank, but he felt strongly about the importance of elevating the Enterprise brand to a higher level. In his usual style, however, Jack worked with the group to come up with an annual per-car expense allowance ($6 for each vehicle in the fleet) that would be used to fund the effort.

As a result, the primary goal of Enterprise's first ad campaign was to increase the number of customers willing to consider Enterprise for their future hometown rental car needs. It remains the company's objective today.

Research determined that Enterprise's pick-up service was a compelling attribute and the greatest differentiator separating the company from its competitors. It was also a message that could be told through advertising. Enterprise concluded that there were a couple of things potential customers needed to know in order to get them to call the company first: Enterprise would pick you up, and its locations were nearby. In other words, easy and convenient.

What's more, Jack decided that the first commercial should be a tribute to Enterprise employees instead of merely a product pitch. This decision went against the advice of his marketing consultants, but he felt he owed it to those who worked so hard to build the company. "We got where we are today because of the men and women who come to work every morning and open the doors, turn on the lights, wash the cars, and pick our customers up," he told the consultants. "I want our first ad to be a tribute to them, and I want it to honor and dignify these employees."

The new commercial was a departure from Enterprise's past local newspaper advertising strategy. It created quite a buzz with employees, primarily because it underscored the sizable contributions they made.

Jack realized the ad was actually reaching out to several audiences: New potential customers for sure, but also his own employees, along with the current and potential strategic partners he wanted to show that Enterprise was the kind of company they could feel comfortable doing business with.

Later commercials were unveiled featuring an automobile wrapped in brown paper, signifying the special service Enterprise offered. "We'll Pick You Up" became the company's slogan and advertising tagline, and it all came about because an individual employee had the power to make a difference.

As the fleet grew, so did the ad budget, although the cost per vehicle allotted to advertising in the fifteen years since has never changed.

Take Advantage of Market Voids

While the Hertzes and Avises of the world were competing near airport runways, Enterprise was growing by leaps and bounds in American driveways. By the early 1980s, the company's once-core business of leasing started sharing the limelight with the ever-growing rental business. The rental side got so big that what was originally known as Enterprise Leasing (and Executive Leasing before that) officially became Enterprise Rent-A-Car.

"One of Jack's great abilities as a manager is not getting hung up on tradition," says company president Don Ross. "He looked around and saw that our biggest source of revenue was coming from renting cars, and the majority of employees worked in the rent-a-car division. He said, 'Why do we have these signs out front that say Enterprise Leasing? We're Enterprise Rent-A-Car. Let's change the name.' Most people who build something like this from the ground up resist changing what they created. But not Jack."

As the competition fought it out for the business travel market and kept coming up with bright ideas for customer loyalty programs, new Enterprise branches continued to sprout up under everyone's radar screen. The company's offices have long been located in unusual places, from strip malls next to Chinese take-outs and Laundromats, to industrial parks and inside of car dealerships. It's cheap and convenient real estate, and it allowed the company to become the first name stranded motorists—and insurance companies—think of when needing temporary transportation. As Enterprise discovered, no one wants to go all the way to the airport to pick up a car when they can get it from an office located next door to where their vehicle is being repaired instead. Besides, Enterprise decided to earn the loyalty of its customers by showering them with great service rather than through awarding frequent-renter points.

The major players didn't seem to take Enterprise seriously. The company's only competition came from smaller, often poorly funded businesses that quickly fell by the wayside. Most wanted to build a moderate business that could be sold or taken public in order for the founders to make a fast buck. All of this worked to Enterprise's advantage, as it continued to form partnerships with new insurance companies, car dealerships, and body shops. For some two decades, Enterprise pretty much shared the home-city market with many small local and regional competitors, along with an occasional foray by one of the big-name national brands.

Those competitors with centralized management structures had trouble in the fluid world of home-city car rentals. Jack Taylor's well-incentivized, autonomous management teams, by contrast, flourished in this environment.

"I used to own a boat, and several years ago I met a fellow boater who was chairman of a holding company that owned Avis at the time," Jack recalls. "He sat on my boat and said, 'Jack, I understand you are in the car rental business. How many vehicles do you have?'

Back then, we had around 80,000 to 100,000 cars. He was shocked. He said, 'Why don't I know about you guys?' This was the chairman of a company that owned Avis. Apparently, he didn't know we existed, much less how many cars were in our fleet."

Two decades ago, as Enterprise began to accelerate its home-city business, the total car rental industry in the United States was about half its current size and almost completely airport based. Enterprise was still barely a fly on the rental radar screen. Even by 1991, according to *Auto Rental News,* the home-city rental segment made up less than one-third of the airport market.

Since 1991, Enterprise has opened an additional 5,500 branches and added an average of 38,000 cars each year to its fleet. At the same time, the home-city market has grown from $2 billion to almost $10 billion. By contrast, the airport segment has seen almost no growth in the past fifteen years and still totals just $8 billion. The child surpassed the parent while the parent wasn't looking.

Without question, one benefit of being different is that competitors have a hard time seeing what you're up to. It's only in recent years that the bigger national players, such as Hertz and others, have made a serious attempt to open off-airport locations as well. Much of that came following 9/11, when air travel went into a serious decline. Those companies focused on the airport market were left with lots full of unrented cars. At the same time, Enterprise could barely keep up with the demand at its home-city locations. "I think 9/11 got Hertz and some of the other players to look in the mirror and realize the limitations of focusing on the airports," notes one industry observer. "That's really when some of the others decided to start going after the home-city market as well." By then, Enterprise's home-city presence was far-reaching, well developed, and not easy to compete with. Enterprise was the leader and had decades of experience on its side.

While competition in the home-city market has certainly increased in recent years, Enterprise is so far ahead of the game and already has agreements in place with such a large number of business partners, it will be difficult for other companies to gain much traction in the foreseeable future. In essence, the overall rental industry continues to shift toward a segment that was effectively invented by Jack Taylor and the Enterprise team. The company's massive growth is also a testament to the increasing trend of drivers renting vehicles locally to better meet specific lifestyle needs, and using rentals for weekend trips instead of putting extra mileage on their own vehicles. In addition, instead of tying up money in company cars, many corporations now opt to rent (rather than buy or lease) for employees as needed for business purposes. Plus, with heightened airport security and all the hassles of flying in our post-9/11 world, scores of travelers now opt to drive to their destinations instead.

"It's very rewarding to have transformed our industry by building a nearly $10 billion business that simply wasn't there before," says CEO Andy Taylor. "What you're seeing is that American consumers are using rental cars in their hometowns and neighborhoods for many needs beyond replacements for automobiles that are in the shop. They're renting for corporate and leisure needs, driving vacations, an extra vehicle, or a different kind of car."

There's an interesting side note to this home-city-market story: Enterprise itself began opening airport offices about a decade ago and today already has about a 7 percent to 8 percent share of the U.S. airport market segment. Although it remains a small part of its business, the airport market has grown to represent 10 percent of the company's overall revenue in just a short span of years. Enterprise now has more than 220 airport locations covering all major cities and has earned J.D. Power and Associates' highest rating in the firm's annual Domestic Airport Rental Car Customer Satisfaction Survey in six of the past seven years. Enterprise continues to prove year in and year out that its unique business model works wherever it is applied because customer service remains at the core of the company's operations.

Conquer New Markets

Today, Enterprise operates several other auto-related businesses—leasing (or fleet services), retail used car sales, and commercial truck rentals—all of which are run under the same principles.

Enterprise is unique in how it obtains and manages its rental fleet. Rather than leasing cars from automakers like most of the competition, Enterprise buys its cars outright. This way of purchasing vehicles, combined with the size of Enterprise's annual car buy, allows it to gain a cost advantage that continues to pay dividends all the way through to the time when the company sells or remarkets the cars. Today, Enterprise has grown to become the largest seller of used cars in the United States.

Most of its vehicles are sold through the remarketing division, which determines the optimal time to put the cars back into the market. Since Enterprise buys virtually all of its rental vehicles from manufacturers, accepting 100 percent risk, the remarketing group is charged with selling back hundreds of thousands of cars a year. Their job is essential, since proceeds from these sales are used to help fund the purchase of new vehicles. Above all, the remarketers must determine the best time and means for selling these cars so that Enterprise gets the highest return possible. By working hard to earn an extra $50 from each sale, multiplied by the incredibly large number of cars sold, it can make a huge difference in the level of profits generated by the company in any given year. This approach gives Enterprise tremendous flexibility to keep vehicles for a shorter or longer period of time, depending on market conditions. For instance, if demand for the Ford Taurus suddenly turns hot, remarketers can start unloading Enterprise's inventory of this model right away to secure a higher return.

Roughly 60 percent of Enterprise's vehicles are sold back to the franchised car dealerships they are bought from by the remarketing group. Another 20 percent go to auto auctions, 10 percent to 12 percent are sold through individual lots for salvage (those involved in accidents), while the remaining 8 percent are sold directly to customers on Enterprise lots through the referral car sales division.

The remarketing department is so good at what it does, it takes only an average of sixteen days for Enterprise to remove a car from service and receive cash from the sales transaction. Not only does the remarketing department help to maximize Enterprise's return on each car sale, it also provides yet another career trajectory for company employees. There are more than 800 people working as remarketing professionals at Enterprise, giving the company the best possible pulse on how, when, and for how much cars should be sold back into the marketplace.

Don't Haggle

Further bucking traditional practices, the way Enterprise sells cars to retail buyers through its referral sales division is also very different. Instead of negotiating on price with buyers, as almost every other car dealership does, Enterprise offers its vehicles for a flat fee, below Kelly Blue Book prices. There are no exceptions—ever. Jack Taylor believes in this "no-haggle" concept to a fault. He's convinced it is what customers desire, and he wants everyone to be treated the same.

"Long before Saturn and others came along with this approach, Enterprise had a one-price system, which was really hard for people to understand at first," says Ross. "People were so used to negotiating, they would really struggle with it. But it taught me a very important lesson about ethics and Jack's commitment to conducting business with integrity. Early on, I got paid a commission of about $15 on each car sold. This guy came in to buy a car one day, and he just wouldn't agree to the deal unless we took something off the price. He said, 'Just give me $5 off and I'll take it.' I went in to my manager and told him he could take the $5 out of my commission, because I wanted to close the sale. We both called Jack to see if that was okay. Jack said, 'No, that's not our deal. Our deal is that we give a fair price and you shouldn't have to give up any of your commission. I hope the customer will respect you for that, but if he doesn't, at least he'll leave saying that while I didn't buy a car from those guys, they're good guys and I'd be willing to come back here again.' The man didn't buy the car, but Jack sure did leave me with a valuable lesson that I still remember vividly to this day."

"Jack always said 'I just don't want to fight with my customers over price,'" adds Andy Taylor. "'I don't want customer A paying more than customer B for the same thing. That's just not fair.'"

Likewise, contrary to industry practice, Enterprise offers a free one-year limited warranty with each used vehicle, and a seven-day "no questions asked" money-back guarantee. Plus, any added services, products, or loan arrangements are priced off of a set menu that applies to all customers.

"You can bring it back within this seven-day period and get a refund even if you don't like the color," says Andy Taylor. "Rather than competing on price, we're trying to win people over by having an overwhelmingly attractive offering. You get the certainty of knowing you are buying a good car and that we stand behind it. If, for whatever reason, the car turns out to be bad, we'll gladly take it back, because our reputation is worth far more than the price of the vehicle."

Enterprise refers to its retail car unit as the "referral sales" division because, in the beginning, it really was based on referrals by friends and family. Jack also felt there were stigmas attached to the word "used," not the least of which were the questionable business practices of some used car lots.

Whatever it's called, by treating all customers as equals, Enterprise has changed the definition for how used cars—and related services—are most effectively sold.

THE ENTERPRISE WAY

1. In order to stand out in a crowded industry, the fundamentals of your product or service must be genuinely unique.
2. Always dress professionally and demand the same of those who work for you.
3. Remain open to new opportunities, including those that aren't immediately apparent.
4. Find innovative ways to make use of company resources seven days a week, to keep revenues coming in even during off times.
5. Empower individual employees to make decisions that lead to new ways of doing things, even if they initially appear to be unconventional and unworkable.

6. Look to capture part of the market that the rest of the competition has ignored.

7. Form alliances with businesses that need your product or service by filling a need that also saves them money.

8. The more convenient you make it for customers to reach you, the more likely they will favor you over everyone else.

9. Don't haggle over price. Instead, charge everyone the same fair amount. Then, back the price up with a guarantee and unparalleled good service.

Never Settle for "Satisfied"

ULFILLING FOUNDER JACK Taylor's commitment to customer service was a lot easier when Enterprise was a small, regional business. Most employees knew one another on a first-name basis, and everyone was clear about their mission. Jack himself was a constant presence, always reminding people, "Repeat customers are the quickest way to build a solid business." Jack was able to keep track of who was taking delivery of leased cars and called to thank his customers personally.

"I still get calls today from people who say they were Jack's first customer," Andy says. "Things were very simple then and everyone felt like they were the first customer."

But as the business grew, keeping this focus on customer service ahead of profits became more challenging to consistently execute. It required putting a formalized system in place to relentlessly track customer satisfaction and ultimately hold employees accountable for delivering on the promise.

The system Enterprise wound up building to track customer service has grown into one of the most comprehensive and effective programs of its kind in corporate America. Yet, at its core, it's also one of the simplest.

The company has dubbed the program ESQi—Enterprise Service Quality index. Why the small "i"? As one senior manager explains, "We want to keep the focus on service and quality, not 'index.'"

As we'll see through examining the results and implementation of ESQi, Enterprise learned that "satisfied" isn't good enough. The key to getting customers to come back—and subsequently tell their friends and family positive things about your business—is making sure they're "completely satisfied."

Hold Everyone Accountable

Every Enterprise branch is assigned its own ESQi score. These numbers are then averaged to come up with an overall company number. The ESQi score represents the percentage of customers who report being completely satisfied with their rental experience. ESQi results are continually measured and reported weekly, although they are only considered to be statistically valid when viewed on a monthly and quarterly basis. Every branch, area, and group knows the ESQi of every other branch, area, and group in the company. That number is crucial, because Enterprise uses this measure as a key variable for determining who gets promoted. If your individual branch has an ESQi score that falls below the corporate average and you're in line for a higher management position, you will not move up until your number improves. By the same token, if you're a general manager and your area's ESQi is below average, you're also staying put until things get turned around. It demonstrates the company's relentless commitment to always taking care of its customers.

While ESQi has become the center of attention at Enterprise, it is a relatively recent innovation. For decades, surveying customers was not a formalized process. The management team at Enterprise didn't feel a need to do anything like this, since the assumption was that everything was fine. Customers must be happy, they figured, since the company was growing and profits kept rising. But this perception turned out to be far different from the reality.

The first real effort to get tangible and quantifiable data didn't begin until 1989, when the company aired its initial national television commercial, which depicted an Enterprise employee handing over the keys to what was referred to as the customer's "own car." Follow-up research, long the standard procedure in advertising, was conducted to learn viewers' impressions of the campaign. A handful of customers who had rented from Enterprise before were gathered into a focus group. While they were there, the company also decided to ask a series of questions about their rental experience. Though the commercial got fairly positive feedback, the service provided by Enterprise was, at best, inconsistent. In some cases, it was quite bad. Customers discussed being given dirty cars, complained they weren't picked up when promised, and some expressed general dissatisfaction with how they were treated. Granted, the results were nonscientific and inconclusive, but they raised some serious concerns. It turned out people weren't as happy as the company thought.

Enterprise commissioned more tracking surveys after learning these results. "We need to know how we're doing," Andy Taylor told his team at headquarters. "It's one thing to feel like you know, and it's another to really know."

Too often the results indicated the company was falling short on service and satisfaction. Taking a cue from the late management guru Peter Drucker, who believed "you manage what you measure," Enterprise decided to create a more accurate and consistent way of tracking customer satisfaction. Without a reliable measure of what was happening, the company was left to decipher everyone's own version of reality. It was becoming increasingly clear to everyone that more needed to be done.

"By 1994, we had more than 4,000 branches, and our revenues had grown in the last 10 years from about $200 million to about $2 billion," Andy Taylor says. "We opened a new branch office somewhere in the United States every business day (which is still the case today) and were beginning to expand into international markets. But customer calls, letters, and other feedback told us both the quality and consistency of our service was coming up short." Some were concerned the company was sacrificing quality for growth, which went completely against Jack Taylor's philosophy.

In deciding to more precisely measure what was happening, the company entered territory that had largely been unexplored up to that point. Little research into customer satisfaction—either how to measure it or its impact on business—was readily available, since this was such a new area of focus.

Enterprise could have gone to an outside consulting group with some experience in the field to get help in developing this tracking program. But since the company had traditionally relied upon its own people, it was decided that this project would be handled in the same way. For one thing, in order for a major initiative such as this to be successful, the entire organization had to support it. Keeping it in-house, and developing it in collaboration with operating groups around the country, helped to ensure that everyone felt an ownership stake in the process.

A small team was put together and charged with creating Enterprise's first official customer survey, which was designed to gauge feedback at the highest possible level.

Quantify How You're Doing

How do you really know whether your customers are satisfied? First, you must identify all of the variables that can add or detract from their experience—all the "touchpoints," or potential face-to-face encounters between customer and company that make or break the relationship. To discover what these touchpoints were for Enterprise, extensive field research was conducted in order to catalog the various encounters that could affect a customer's experience. Employees were polled to learn about the questions they thought customers should be asked, and renters were queried directly about what mattered most to them. Similar work was done at the car sales and fleet services levels, to develop customer satisfaction surveys for those areas as well.

The findings backed up what Jack Taylor had long espoused: Satisfying customers is not complicated. It's about doing the right things: smiling, shaking the customer's hand, using a formal greeting with their last name, having a great attitude, and letting people know the company appreciates their business. But new questions kept being added to the draft customer survey, making the job of creating a final version more complicated than originally planned.

After a year of constant refinement, the first formal survey went out in July 1994. It consisted of eighteen questions and was mailed quarterly to a combined 1,600 customers selected at random from every operating group. Customers were asked about all aspects of the Enterprise experience: Were you treated as though you were a valued customer? How satisfied were you with the Enterprise employees you dealt with? With their courtesy? Their professionalism? Their promptness? The selection of cars? The mechanical condition of the vehicle? Its cleanliness, inside and out? The overall price? The time it took to complete the transaction? The pick-up service?

Finally, customers were asked to grade the overall Enterprise experience on a five-point scale, ranging from completely satisfied to completely dissatisfied.

The company hadn't planned to ask so many questions, but its desire to learn as much as possible about what pushed customer buttons led to this larger list of queries. It took a few minutes to complete the survey, which dissuaded many customers from filling it out in the first place. The initial response rate was about 25 percent—not terrible, but not great, either. Surveys were sent out every quarter, and the results consistently showed a significant spread between the groups rated highest in customer satisfaction and those rated the lowest. The conclusion was unmistakable to Andy Taylor. "It proved that customer satisfaction wasn't necessarily top-of-mind with all employees at every Enterprise branch office," he says.

Still, many veteran managers didn't think anything needed to be fixed. With revenues at an all-time high, they questioned the validity of the survey results, especially since there were no definitive data linking satisfaction scores to the company's bottom-line performance.

"Quite honestly, in the early days we measured how well we were taking care of our customers by how much our business had grown," says company president Don Ross. "It was a pretty informal and anecdotal process, and we didn't really have a way to solidify how we were doing."

Nevertheless, top executives at headquarters couldn't ignore the limitations of this mail-in survey. For one thing, by the time the results were returned and could be properly tabulated, it was too late to provide meaningful, timely feedback to the group. Furthermore, they realized that the sheer number of questions might be influencing the results and therefore reducing the response rate. Plus, if the survey only drilled down to the group level, how could managers know what was going on at an individual branch, where the real improvements needed to be made? And, given that no one was being held accountable or penalized for poor results, how could managers even start to fix any problems?

Top-Box Only, Please

At a general managers meeting in 1996, the idea of taking the survey down to the individual branch level was first broached. Some skeptics in the room questioned whether this was a worthwhile effort. Branches, groups, and regions are all responsible for their own expenses. Since compensation is based on profitability, there's a lot of pressure to keep budgets under control. The basic group-level survey cost $350,000 annually. Taking it to the branch level would be ten times more expensive—$3.5 million per year. Many groups continued to question whether the surveys were worth anything at all. Therefore, a test was proposed.

"We asked people who said they knew how their branches would perform to give us a list and tell us what the score would be for each location," Ross explains. A customer satisfaction survey was sent out specifically for customers of those individual branches. The results? Managers who predicted which branches would have high or low scores were right 50 percent of the time. In other words, the same odds as flipping a coin.

Skeptics of the program were mostly silenced by these results, and the surveys were promptly expanded to every branch. But this time the company decided to do something a bit different. Instead of mailing out questionnaires, the surveys would now be conducted by an outside market research firm and done by phone. This was designed to get faster feedback and help to increase response rates, since customers only had to spend a few minutes talking to a representative rather than going through the hassle of filling out a lengthy card. As an added benefit, by using an outside company, the results and responses would be more objective. (There was no risk, for example, that the questioner might try to talk a customer into changing their answer.)

In the beginning, the company kept all eighteen questions on the phone survey. This proved to be a disaster, since customers didn't want to spend that much time talking to the survey takers. "They said, 'Why are you asking us so many questions?'" chief operating officer Pam Nicholson recalls.

With that in mind, the number of survey questions was cut down to just two: One, "How would you rate your overall experience?" using the same five-point scale that consisted of completely satisfied, satisfied, somewhat satisfied, somewhat dissatisfied, and completely dissatisfied. Two, "Would you consider renting from Enterprise again?"

"We wanted to get an overall measure of customer satisfaction and a clear indication of whether people would do business with us again," says Andy Taylor.

The questions were simple enough, but the results spoke volumes.

When ESQi was first rolled out, many general managers thought their branches would come out at the very top of the charts. But some of the most confident ones learned the truth: They weren't doing a very good job. "The first thing I wanted to say was, 'The measurement is off!' I thought customers loved us," recalls one general manager. "But they didn't feel as good as I thought."

By the mid-1990s, Enterprise's ESQi experiment was in full swing. The more the company learned about its "completely satisfied" customers, the more it recognized their importance.

Most businesses that conduct customer satisfaction surveys put respondents who report being "satisfied" or "completely satisfied" together in one group. But subsequent research conducted by Enterprise found there was a huge difference between the two categories. More than 70 percent of those in the "completely satisfied" category said they would definitely use Enterprise again the next time they rented a car. By contrast, only 22 percent of "satisfied" customers vowed to come back. The company then checked intentions against actual behavior and found that "top-box" customers—that is, those who reported the highest customer satisfaction ratings—were, in fact, repeat customers. The merely "satisfied" were not nearly as likely to ever return. That information hit company leaders like a lightning bolt. "This showed—once and for all—that customer satisfaction isn't one of those 'soft' management issues," Andy Taylor concluded. "It has a direct impact on the bottom line." Suddenly, the $3.5 million annual cost of conducting the ESQi survey seemed like a bargain.

Enterprise finally had the proof that some of its high-flying managers demanded—namely, a direct link between customer satisfaction and the bottom line. Even though the survey now asked only two general questions, the company learned more than it ever did through its tedious multiquestion mail-in surveys. "Our employees, the timeliness of the transaction, and the condition of our cars are absolutely the three drivers of ESQi," says Ross. "When numbers go south or get out of whack, it's usually because one of those things went wrong."

By backtracking the dates and times of any transactions in question, the company can determine whether, for example, a less than completely satisfied customer came to a branch when it was short-staffed, or on a day with a diminished selection of cars. Now Enterprise would know for certain how good it was at satisfying customers at each of its branches, instead of relying on flawed assumptions. Unfortunately, the company was unsure how to use ESQi to drive day-to-day actions, since there were really no formalized repercussions for those working at or managing the underperforming offices. As a first step, Enterprise formed a standards committee and began sharing best practices from top-performing branches with the rest of the company. But there was clearly more that needed to be done.

Hold Everyone Accountable

Every year the company holds a multiday officers meeting for senior managers. It's an opportunity to reflect on what the company has accomplished over the past year, look ahead to future goals, and socialize with peers. At the October 1996 event, held at Turnberry Isle, Florida, there was a lot to celebrate. Enterprise was coming off of its best year ever and had just passed Hertz to become the largest rental car company in the United States. What's more, the approach for measuring ESQi had finally been greatly refined, and the results of the latest survey would be announced at the gathering.

However, the celebratory mood in the grand ballroom quickly evaporated as the numbers were revealed. That's because the scores came in below projected targets across the board. A wide gap still existed between the best- and worst-performing branches. Most troublesome of all, insurance adjusters, a key company customer group, not only gave Enterprise low customer satisfaction scores, they actually rated it below a major competitor. When the graphic illustrating this fact was displayed, Jack Taylor, seated in the back, became noticeably upset.

"Andrew," he said to his son as soon as the meeting concluded, "we've got a big problem."

"It certainly got my attention," Andy Taylor recalls, "because he hadn't called me 'Andrew' in about thirty years. And I knew from childhood that when he said 'Andrew,' it usually meant, at a minimum, 'Listen very carefully to what I am about to say.' He was visibly upset. He told me that Enterprise, which had grown way, way beyond what we had ever expected, was now in danger of losing touch with the core value that was the foundation of its success."

That evening, calling the ESQi results "a slap in the face," Jack challenged company leaders to turn those numbers around. A decision was immediately reached to make ESQi the foremost measure by which the company was managed. As a first step, ESQi scores were incorporated as one of the primary factors used to determine the winners of the annual President's and Chairman's Awards, the company's most prestigious honors for operating groups. Among senior managers, these are highly coveted recognitions. Recipients of the awards, which are handed out once a year, had historically been chosen based on the growth and profitability experienced by their respective branches. No longer. Now, to even be eligible, having an above-average ESQi score was a must.

Winning one of these awards didn't just mean receiving a nice plaque to hang up in the office. It was, and is, virtually a guarantee of career advancement at the company. Some of the folks who were winning year in and year out were now shown to have some of the worst customer satisfaction scores. If they failed to raise their ESQi score above the company's average, they would be ineligible for these honors going forward. As insiders at the company put it, those who didn't measure up were sent to "ESQi jail." The only way to get out was by doing a much better job of taking care of customers.

The company's renewed commitment was evident at the officers meeting the following year. Some of the perennial winners did not receive awards. "That was huge in our world," Andy Taylor recalls. "Nobody could remember the last time those top performers had been shut out. They were doing a lot of things well, but they were not making enough of their customers happy. As a result, they were no longer recognized as being truly the best at Enterprise."

There was anger and grumbling from some who found themselves brought down by poor ESQi scores. Others contended the measurement was unfair. They argued it was harder to please a customer in, say, Los Angeles or New York City than in Mobile, Alabama, where folks presumably weren't as demanding and the pace of life was slower. But Andy Taylor and others in senior management disagreed and could point to individual branches within these underperforming groups that showed exceptional customer satisfaction scores. And, given how the survey was conducted, it was nearly impossible for any group to fudge the numbers.

Determined to get managers to take the scores even more seriously, ESQi was then made part of the formula used to determine promotability. From that point on, the only way to move ahead in the company, and therefore make more money, was to see that your branch or operating group had top-box ESQi scores.

"We made a big deal out of the numbers," Andy Taylor says. "We posted scores prominently in our monthly operating reports, right next to the profit numbers that determine managers' pay. Operating managers could see how well they and their peers were doing because everyone was ranked from top to bottom."

The biggest wake-up call of the importance these numbers held came in 1998, when a prominent group vice president who always posted outstanding financial results was passed over for a promotion because of his group's low ESQi scores. Says Andy, "He kept his expenses low by not having enough employees, and they were getting burned out. At the same time, he tried to sell customers add-ons they didn't need. While he was making a large amount of money, he received terrible customer satisfaction ratings. When we refused to promote him, it got everyone's attention and sent a clear message that ESQi is for real." Some otherwise high performers left the company after not being promoted. While this caused some short-term pain for the company, executives say the ensuing benefits were well worth it.

The ESQi score for the company overall climbed from 67 percent in 1994 to 72 percent in 1998. Today it hovers around 80 percent. "We broke the 80 barrier for the first time in early 2006," Andy Taylor observes.

When ESQi was first adopted, there was a 28-point gap between the best and worst group scores. Today that gap has been cut to around 9 points. This put to rest any doubts about the effectiveness of the program. It also dispelled some widespread myths about what it takes to make customers happy:

MYTH #1: *Boosting customer satisfaction requires giving away the store.*

There was an initial fear that local branch managers would rely on giveaways to "buy" happy customers, sacrificing profits for increased scores. But the company's research showed that outstanding overall service, not giveaways, led to higher scores. In fact, since ESQi was first measured, the most profitable groups have also had some of the highest ESQi scores.

MYTH #2: *Good managers already know which areas need improvement.*

Some general managers like to manage by gut instinct and "feel." But, as Enterprise proved by comparing the managers' intuitive conclusions with actual survey results, there is no substitute for statistically valid measurements. And without these measurements, it's impossible to manage knowledgeably and effectively.

MYTH #3: *There's not much difference between being somewhat satisfied and being completely satisfied.*

Enterprise proved by tracking both survey results and subsequent behavior that completely satisfied customers are *three times* more likely to do business with you again than those who are somewhat satisfied. "Completely satisfied customers are often predisposed to using you again without even checking with a competitior because they know they'll get a quality service and good value from you," Ross observes.

MYTH #4: *Complete satisfaction means perfection.*

Perfection is something to strive for, but it's rarely ever attained. Besides, a customer may have encountered significant problems in the transaction yet still report being completely satisfied, provided the problems are taken care of appropriately. As one example, Andy Taylor cites a letter he received from a customer who held premier status with all of the major car rental companies over the past thirty years. (Enterprise has no such program.)

"I generally view them [loyalty programs] as commodities because that is how they treat their customers, regardless of their past loyalty," the customer wrote. "So, in these days of 'Customer No Service,' it is refreshing to experience the following: To be offered cold drinks on a hot summer day; To be recognized and addressed properly by your last name, pronounced correctly, by the way; To be telephoned the day after you rent a car just to make sure everything was okay; And to be treated in an extremely professional and personable manner during the entire experience."

The kicker is that this particular customer was put in three different cars because he wasn't satisfied with the first two. But owing to the way the situation was handled, he was completely satisfied with the experience. In his letter he recommended the branch manager be given a promotion. She ultimately was.

Identify Characteristics of Top Performers

So what is it that "top-box" managers do? What are their secrets to completely satisfying customers? While developing the company's customer service training modules, company executives met with many of the highest performers to find out, though they offered little insight. Eventually, the company realized it was asking the wrong questions. Instead, Enterprise executives decided to study these top-box managers to see exactly how they spent their days.

In doing so, the secret to great customer service came pouring out. Top-box managers concentrated on visiting branches and meeting directly with employees. At all of these meetings, the first and last thing the managers talked about was customer service.

They stressed the need to be good to customers because they were the lifeblood of the company's growth.

All of the high performers made a focus on customer service the priority in their meetings with employees—asking how the customers were doing and finding out what steps employees were taking to meet their needs.

Make Pleasing Customers a Habit

ESQi and what it represents have become a way of life at Enterprise. Managers don't necessarily wait for their ESQi scores to find out how they're doing in the area of customer satisfaction. They make it a daily habit, hoping to ingrain these philosophies into the entire team's culture. "You can easily spot the high performers," Andy Taylor adds. "They're the ones who 'get it.' They have high ESQi scores, retention, and profits. And they have fun in the process. Ask yourself if your culture is like this. If not, what can you change in yourself to help your team perform better overall?"

The most successful leaders walk in every morning asking, "How happy are our customers and what can I do to help?" In addition, they hire smart people and allow managers and employees in the branches to fix problems on the spot. In other words, they give each individual the power to make things right with the customer.

To ensure complete satisfaction, when a customer returns a car to Enterprise, before being checked out, he or she is asked two key questions: "How was our service?" and "What could we have done to make your experience better?" If a customer expresses even the slightest dissatisfaction, employees are taught to say, "I'm sorry" and ask what they can do to fix the problem.

Let's say your car was dirty or didn't operate properly. If you bring that to the Enterprise employee's attention, in addition to fixing the problem, they might offer you a discount on a future visit or find another way to make amends. Just acknowledging the problem and apologizing can do wonders in terms of a customer's experience. People want to know they have been heard and their concerns have been addressed. Every branch is even required to commit part of its operating budget to writing off losses involved with making whatever amends are necessary to keep a customer happy. It's what's known as the customer satisfaction account. "From the day they hit the counter at the branch, our people have the ability to give something away if they need to without getting any additional approval," Nicholson notes.

In such cases, Enterprise managers are trained to give customers a full bill of charges, then make it clear in black and white what discounts are being applied as compensation for any inconvenience. For instance, let's say a customer booked a three-day rental and is going to be rebated back for one of those days because of a service problem. The final bill would still show the charges for the full three-day rental, followed by a breakdown of the adjustment being offered. The reason for doing this, as opposed to just charging a lower amount, is that it allows the customer to see the value of the compensation being offered by the company in black and white. It also makes it clear to the branch—and corporate office—how much not taking proper care of customers is draining from overall profits. This is yet another way the company quantifies the cost of failing to keep customers happy.

Perhaps not surprisingly, there's an inverse relationship between customer satisfaction account budgets and ESQi scores. In other words, branches spending the most on customer satisfaction generally have the lowest ESQi scores. The reason? High-performing branches do things right the first time and therefore have no need to dig into this account to make amends.

Nevertheless, offering to resolve problems the moment they are brought up can frequently transform an unhappy customer into one that is completely satisfied. It can also turn someone who never wants to do business with you again into a loyal fan.

But let's say a customer doesn't leave the Enterprise branch happy and expresses his or her dissatisfaction when called by the outside service to discuss their experience with the company. If the response to the first question is anything but "completely satisfied," the customer is asked whether someone from the branch can follow up to rectify the situation. "The survey takers are trained to ask if there is anything Enterprise could do and whether it would be all right for one of our managers to call them," Ross explains. "If the customer says he or she would like to speak with a manager, the manager of the branch where the customer rented from will call within forty-eight hours. Not only are managers required to call, they also have to report back to their management with the results of that call."

"It's important for us to find out why customers are unhappy and do what it takes to make things right," Jack Taylor adds.

Granted, there are times when customers simply can't be pleased, and Enterprise isn't always perfect. Sometimes employees are late in picking people up, and if that causes a customer to be late for an appointment, there might not be anything you can do to push them into the "completely satisfied" column. The point is, the company knows it must make a valiant effort to bring customers to that top-box level, since the cost of not doing so is so great.

"We don't see top-box customer satisfaction as an extravagance," Andy Taylor adds. "Rather, it's the cornerstone of our business model."

The ESQi gathering process does have its potential flaws. For instance, if an employee knows that a particular customer is unhappy and he or she has been unable to move the customer to the "completely satisfied" category for whatever reason, the employee could write down a false phone number on the final bill, making it impossible for the outside calling service to reach the person. This happened more frequently in the early days of the program. Today, various checks have been put into place to stop the practice. For instance, a computerized system verifies the contact phone number being used for each customer throughout the rental process. If the initial number entered into the system suddenly changes when the transaction is closed out, it gets flagged. Executives also receive a printout of all undialable and/or unreachable numbers each month and follow up on these with the branch. Any such dishonest action by an employee can lead to termination.

While no system is faultless, Ross believes that businesses of all sizes are well served by surveying customers. "Unless you have a measurement, you never really know how you're doing," he says.

Fortunately, it's not necessary for smaller companies to spend millions of dollars, as Enterprise does, on tracking customer service. One of the best ways to survey customers is by having employees ask how everything was at the end of every transaction. "Beyond that, I would ask three critical questions," Ross offers. "The overall question: How satisfied were you? The second question should be more open-ended: What could we have done to improve our service? And the third question: What do you think we do especially well?" Ross recommends that surveys beyond those taken in person always be conducted by phone rather than mail, based on Enterprise's extensive research into the subject.

Always Aim Higher

Enterprise continually strives to move its overall ESQi scores higher. While 100 percent is the ultimate goal, surpassing 80 was a major accomplishment. "Perfecting customer service is always in a mode of constant improvement," Ross points out. "In fact, it's almost the kiss of death when someone says, 'I've got it!' because you are constantly looking for ways to take even better care of your customers." Interestingly enough, the company's ESQi scores in most international markets are often higher than in the United States, largely because the home-city car rental business is newer in those regions and the high level of customer service offered by Enterprise is so unusual. New branches in North America also tend to score higher than older ones, since employees are motivated to work harder and treat customers better as they get their businesses up and running.

Through its ESQi surveys, Enterprise has identified six attributes that have the greatest impact on customer satisfaction. They are:

- Satisfaction with personal courtesy.
- Satisfaction with personal professionalism.
- Satisfaction with personal timeliness of service.
- Satisfaction with personal treatment as a valued customer.
- Satisfaction with the mechanical condition of the car.
- Satisfaction with the timeliness to complete the rental transaction.

As you can see, most of these attributes have to do with service rather than with the quality of the product. And service is something every company can address. By concentrating on these attributes, groups can raise their ESQi scores. Negatives in any area are destructive to overall customer satisfaction.

It's possible for any branch to improve its ESQi score. Many have come up with unique ways of doing so. For instance, several years ago, a group rental manager in the United Kingdom asked his employees, "What do you think your ESQi should be?" Everyone threw out a number that was greater than the group's actual score. The manager wondered why there was such a discrepancy.

In response, he developed a new system called "The Vote," which is now used at branches around the world. This system holds each employee accountable for the branch's ESQi score through an organized ranking process. Once a week, coworkers publicly rank everyone in the office from top to bottom based on their customer service efforts during the week. They must also explain the rationale for these rankings to help those with lower numbers learn what they need to do to improve. "We weren't listening to each other as a team," Andy Taylor says. "Everyone needs to work together as a branch to be effective. 'The Vote' is a way of making the entire team responsible for each individual's behavior through constructive criticism."

The Vote system is most successful when critiques are kept to a constructive level, so that employees don't take them personally and start breeding resentment. Often, the take-away is to stick with those objective things that are immediately noticeable—such as more smiles and faster service. Another goal? Get everyone to emulate the traits of top-ranking performers.

Likewise, many branches keep what's dubbed a "Success/Failure Log." This is a day-to-day recording of what things went right and wrong at the office in each area of the operation. Every employee has access to the log and is encouraged to make entries in it. For instance, if a customer was particularly dissatisfied with a certain aspect of the experience, or an employee solved a problem for a business partner in an especially effective way, this could be noted in the log.

The log, which is also available to managers throughout the operating group, is an excellent diagnostic tool for spotting trends and service issues. In addition, like The Vote, it allows everyone to learn from the successes and failures of others.

Enterprise claims that those branches scoring highest on customer service do so by taking the rental process from *transaction* to *interaction*. In other words, instead of being transaction based, they view the rental experience as an opportunity to build relationships with customers.

To understand the concept in its simplest form, think about your last experience at a fast food drive-thru window. You hand over your money, and the cashier gives you a sandwich. It's purely transaction based. Compare that to walking into a place like Enterprise that appreciates your business, shakes your hand when you walk in, and greets you by name. That is the sort of establishment you feel good about going to. "Even if our prices go up, you'll still want to come back because our people are good to you and you have a relationship with them," Andy Taylor says.

Touch Customers Throughout the Cycle of Service

Like every business, Enterprise has multiple opportunities to impact a customer's experience. It's what Enterprise calls its "Cycle of Service"—moments of truth that give the company a chance to differentiate itself from the competition. Each step of the cycle has an influence on both the branch's overall ESQi score and the customer's perception of the company.

To exceed customer expectations at each step in the cycle, Enterprise focuses on branch staffing, operational plans, and employee training. It's what might be compared to the factors of a winning sports team. To have a world-class, championship-caliber team, you need quality players. This depth is what allows

you to win week in and week out and is the *staffing* part of the
equation. You have to have a great game plan, and a solid play-
book gives you the right plays for the right situations. This is the
planning. And then it takes practice. Even the greatest team, with
the best players and game plan, has to practice. This, of course,
is the *training*. The team's task is to be prepared to execute flaw-
lessly during crunch time.

To better understand how employees can impact each of these
moments of truth, or stops along the Cycle of Service, let's take a
look at how each one applies at Enterprise.

The Telephone
This is often the first contact a customer has with any company,
be it to get information or to make an appointment to come in.
How many times does the phone ring before it is answered? Are
customers put on hold? How are they greeted? Are you making
the sale before hanging up? First impressions are crucial, and
they often come by phone. Enterprise trains its employees not to
let the phone ring more than twice before it is answered. When
they pick up the line, they are told to speak clearly, use a consistent greeting, give their name, and smile. (That's right, customers
can "hear" you smile.)

The Pick-up
More than most companies, Enterprise has a perfect opportunity
to build relationships with customers during the pick-up. This
represents their first face-to-face meeting, as customers are driven
to the rental office to retrieve their loaner vehicle. "A smile, a
handshake, eye-to-eye contact, and using the customer's name is
imperative, whether it's during a pick-up, a delivery, at the dealership, or in our lobby," notes an Enterprise city manager in

Montgomery, Alabama. "This gives the business a personal touch, showing the customer we want their business, and it sets us apart from the competition." It's also essential to always be on time, let customers know when their ride is on the way, open the car door, help load any personal items, and begin building a rapport with friendly chitchat during the drive to the branch.

Branch Arrival

The ultimate goal is for every customer to be treated like a family member, not a number. The amount of time spent in line should be kept to a minimum. It's important to thoroughly explain the entire rental process, including extra fees and late charges that might apply, to avoid any surprises at the end. Customers also need to know whom to call with any questions or problems. "We do simple things like hand the customer a business card at the beginning of the rental process," says a city manager from Louisville, Kentucky. "We let the customer know that if there's a problem, they should feel free to call and it will be corrected. We take pride in being ourselves and making the whole process go as smoothly as possible."

The Rental Contract

Everyone likes to know what they are signing, but few of us have time to actually read through the very small print on a car rental contract. That's why Enterprise employees are trained to go over every important aspect of the agreement with customers, so they are clear about the document's provisions. "When we thoroughly explain the rental process, our customers aren't surprised and they're happier," notes an area manager from Boston. "We don't want them to think that we're giving them services or products they don't really want."

The Car

In addition to having a clean, well-presented appearance, Enterprise employees make sure customers understand how their assigned car operates. It's important to explain how the headlights, seat belts, and wipers work (even if it's not raining), since no one likes surprises. Before sending them on their way, employees show customers exactly how to get out of the lot and offer directions to further enhance this moment of truth.

Callbacks and Switchouts

Among the services offered by Enterprise is following up with body and service shops to see when customer vehicles will be ready. These are known as callbacks. It's crucial for Enterprise employees to keep customers updated on the status of their vehicles, so they feel that the company is looking out for them. By the same token, if a customer walks in expecting to get a Lincoln and walks out with a Neon because that's the only car in stock, employees are encouraged to do their best to switch customers into the specific model they want when it becomes available. Knowing these preferences and making the switchout process as seamless as possible can make customers forget about any disappointment they felt upon getting the wrong vehicle in the first place.

Returning the Vehicle

When customers bring the car back, it's important to make them feel welcome. In addition to handling the return quickly and efficiently, Enterprise employees again shake the customer's hand, smile, and ask about the rental experience. By now a rapport has been built, which will likely make the customer feel free to express an honest opinion about the experience, even if they weren't totally happy about something. That way, the situation can be taken care of, helping to move the person to the completely satisfied category. At the end of the process, employees utter two crucial words: "Thank you."

Invitation to Return

Before a customer leaves, Enterprise employees offer a friendly reminder about how the company can meet all of their future rental needs, while mentioning the other specialty services offered by the company (including car sales and fleet services).

Completely Satisfied Customer

This, of course, is the ultimate goal. One way to get there is by always being proactive. "Instead of waiting for a customer to tell us they're unhappy, we try to sense their unhappiness and ask them what we can do to make it better," says one area manager.

WHY CUSTOMERS DON'T COMPLAIN

One reason it's hard for companies to know what to fix is that customers don't always tell you how they really feel. Enterprise has found there are several reasons why customers are reluctant to speak up:

1. They fear it won't do any good.
2. They think complaining is difficult.
3. They feel awkward about saying anything negative.
4. There is plenty of competition, so it's easy for them to just bring their business elsewhere.

Put Yourself in Your Customer's Shoes

Among the best ways to understand what customers are thinking, and therefore how you can improve their overall experience, is by putting yourself in their shoes.

"I've always been observant of things like that," Jack Taylor says. "I remember before Enterprise was nationwide, I rented a car from another big company during a trip to New York. They charged twice what was supposed to be the special rate. When I questioned the person at the counter about it, she turned around, grabbed a piece of paper, put it in my face, and said, 'Prices are controlled by the city of New York, so you'll have to contact them if you have a problem with it.' I sat there in shock and thought to myself that if this were my business, I'd never treat my customer like that. Why should a customer have to write some big government agency to discuss a price special that was clearly advertised by the car rental company?"

Enterprise teaches its employees that observation is one of the best ways to learn what needs to be improved throughout every division in the company. Workers at all levels are encouraged to constantly look around the office, hear how many times the phone rings before being picked up, look at the expressions on the faces of customers and other teammates to see whether they are smiling or showing signs of frustration, and make sure to properly greet everyone coming through the door.

In sum, Enterprise has learned through all of the processes outlined in this chapter that creating a completely satisfied customer doesn't just happen by accident. It's a deliberate process that requires a continuous commitment, frequent training, constant monitoring, and financial consequences for those who don't live up to the high standards of service. At the same time, the foundation is built upon those common courtesies we all expect. It really comes down to the golden rule of treating your customers the way you would want to be treated yourself.

"When you think about it, we're actually not in the car rental business at all," adds Andy Taylor. "We're in the customer satisfaction business. And that's a trait we have in common with every successful service company, large or small."

THE ENTERPRISE WAY

1. The only way to know how you're really doing when it comes to taking care of your customers is to ask them.

2. It's essential to regularly survey customers about the various aspects of your business. The best way to do this is in person. Any follow-up interviews should be done by phone rather than in writing.

3. If you're going to conduct a survey, make it targeted. If you have more than one office, ensure that you are gathering data specific to each location. Then average these results to get a number for the company as a whole.

4. Ask customers three critical questions: How satisfied were you? What could we have done to improve our service? What do you think we do especially well?

5. Hold everyone accountable for getting your customer satisfaction numbers higher. The way to do that is by tying promotional potential—and therefore compensation advancement—directly in to these results.

6. Measure customer satisfaction at least monthly, and do it consistently to make sure the numbers are improving and that frontline teams have current results.

7. Outstanding service, not giveways, is what results in happy customers.

8. Completely satisfied customers are *three times* more likely to do business with you again than those who are somewhat satisfied.

9. You don't have to be perfect for customers to be completely satisfied; you just have to handle any problems promptly and appropriately.

10. Identify the characteristics of your top performers and use them as an example for everyone else in the organization to follow.

11. Make pleasing customers a way of life and a daily habit that becomes part of the overall culture.

12. Always aim to improve the delivery of customer service to an ever-higher level.

13. Be certain to touch customers throughout the entire Cycle of Service.

14. To better understand how your customers feel and perceive your company, put yourself in their shoes.

15. Realize that customers don't become completely satisfied by accident. It's a deliberate process that requires continuous commitment, frequent training, constant monitoring, and financial consequences for those who don't measure up.

4

Hire and Train Good People from the Ground Up

IMAGINE YOU'RE A new college graduate, ready to enter the workforce and take on the world. You go speak to a recruiter and are told about an entry-level management job with a major company. While you'll have to start at the bottom, you're assured the position has tremendous upside potential. The company will teach you how to run your own business. Then, after getting this training, you'll have a chance to run the business, with full responsibility for pricing, hiring, training, and all other aspects of the operation. You'll share in the profits of the company, yet you won't have to put a dime of your own money on the table to get started. As you do well, you'll make even more. Before long, you won't have just one branch, but five, and perhaps even dozens more under you down the line.

Sound too good to be true? Well, that's exactly the pitch Enterprise has long offered to its new recruits, the majority of whom know absolutely nothing about the car rental industry upon joining the company.

"I've always wanted to start with a totally blank sheet of paper," says Jack Taylor, summing up his hiring philosophy. "For instance, if you bring on an automobile salesman who is used to high- or lowballing during negotiations, and who employs the T.O. ("take-over") sales tactic, it's tough to break them out of that habit. But if you take an inexperienced person, you've got an unfettered mind that you can teach the proper ways you want things done."

Jack discovered that if he chose the right people, previous experience didn't matter. In the early days, he didn't even have a specific blueprint for his people to follow. They were allowed to make much of it up as they went along. Jack simply preached the gospel of customer service, and as long as employees acted accordingly—even if they made costly mistakes that later proved to be valuable lessons—he was satisfied. As Enterprise has clearly demonstrated, given the tools and support necessary to make decisions and accept responsibility, people of all backgrounds are capable of extraordinary achievements.

Most of the original Enterprise employees came to the company through word of mouth. Either they heard about a growing business that was on the lookout for sharp, friendly workers, or they somehow came to the attention of Jack or his people and were recruited directly. Acquaintances and friends of friends with no background in the business, and no claims of expertise, fueled the company's growth as it evolved from a local auto-leasing operation into a quiet rental giant.

Much has changed since those early days in terms of how Enterprise finds qualified candidates, but the traits it looks for in its people remain largely the same. Enterprise's growth has given it a voracious appetite for fresh, career-oriented people, and the company now has a comprehensive recruitment program. Enterprise hires thousands of candidates a year for its management training program. Staying true to the idea of having a clean slate to work with, a majority of all hires fall into one of two categories: recent university graduates or people wanting to begin a new career in a structured management training program. Indeed, Enterprise has emerged as one of the largest recruiters of new college graduates in the United States.

Enterprise takes on graduates from a variety of academic backgrounds. A business degree isn't required, since the company teaches all new hires everything they need to know through its in-depth training program.

Enterprise has more than 200 recruiters, the majority of whom work within each of the individual operating groups or regions around the world. A small staff at headquarters supports these recruiters. Enterprise recruiters are a constant presence at college campuses, even when they don't have urgent openings to fill, since the company wants to remain at the forefront of student minds when it comes time to find a job. Enterprise also finds qualified candidates through its Web site, where potential candidates can learn about the company, view openings, read employee profiles, and apply for a specific job using an online response-based process. Applications are sent electronically directly to the applicable groups in the areas you indicate a desire to work in and are followed up on by recruiters within seven to ten days.

Enterprise also has a paid college internship program, which it compares to "Business 101 on ten cups of coffee or speed-reading through the best business textbooks." The company takes on about 1,700 juniors and seniors each year as interns, teaching them highly marketable skills relating to every aspect of running a successful business. In addition, Enterprise hires a number of hourly and part-time workers to perform support functions such as washing cars and serving as valets in high-volume locations. But 95 percent of the focus on filling full-time positions is spent on bringing people into the entry-level management training program.

What attracts potential candidates to Enterprise? The opportunity to create their own career path; performance-based promotions; autonomy; and the potential for substantial earnings. Positive word of mouth about the culture and the people who work at the company are also important factors.

According to an employee survey, the following are the top reasons (in order) that people choose to work for Enterprise:

1. The opportunity for growth and promotion.
2. The company's excellent reputation.
3. Enterprise's customer-friendly focus.
4. Promotions based on performance rather than seniority.
5. The fact that Enterprise is a growing company and an industry leader.
6. Enterprise's commitment to its employees.
7. The strength of Enterprise's friendly, highly motivated workforce.
8. The company's policy of promoting from within.

Identify Leadership Potential

Renting cars for a living isn't the most glamorous of jobs. In the broad scheme of things, it's generally viewed to be on the lower end of the career and pay spectrum. And that's usually the case. With just about every other rental car company, if you apply for an entry-level job, you'll make a fairly low wage and likely find yourself behind the counter for years, if not the rest of your working life. That's because you're applying for the specific dead-end job just about every rental car company is looking to fill: counterperson.

Enterprise is different. The company doesn't want people who merely seek to be behind the rental counter. It wants every candidate to aspire to greatness. The management trainee position represents a unique career trajectory that can literally take an employee from the ground floor to the executive suite in a matter of years. As a result, Enterprise rarely competes for talent with others in the industry because it doesn't have a lot of opportunities for people who just want to rent cars.

One's career progression at Enterprise works something like this: As a management trainee, a new hire earns a salary that ranges from around $30,000 to $38,000 annually, depending on the region of the country. Within his or her first year to eighteen months, a new recruit will probably have a chance to earn a promotion to management assistant and then assistant branch manager. At this point, in addition to a slightly higher base salary, he or she is paid a portion of the branch's profits. After about two or three years with the company, the employee may then become a branch manager, earning an even bigger share of the overall profits. Total compensation might double from the starting wage. Within five to six years, the next step up is to become an area manager, overseeing three or four branches, earning a percentage of profits from each of those locations. Annual income can exceed $85,000 to $100,000. From here, he or she can become a regional or group rental manager, overseeing three or four areas. Then, depending on geography, he or she might be promoted to either a regional or group vice president. While there are many side trajectories one can go down, the traditional career path would be to become a general manager, a position with the potential to earn a seven-figure compensation package as one of the company's highest performers.

We'll explore Enterprise's entrepreneurial business structure and performance-driven, profit-based compensation program in greater depth in Chapter 5. But the company's core philosophy calls for everyone to start at the bottom and work their way up (with the exception of positions in the corporate office that require a specific skill set, such as a law degree, CPA designation, or technology expertise). Every field management position gets filled from within. General managers are never recruited straight in from the outside world. Each of Enterprise's top executives started at the very bottom, learning what it takes to please a customer, one transaction at a time.

Promote from Within

Enterprise's "work your way up" and "promote from within" policy assures that every field employee at all levels has been fully immersed in the company's culture and way of doing business. Beginning on day one, new hires are thoroughly schooled on the ins and outs of exceeding customer expectations. The structure also guarantees that each person managing those under him or her has spent time in the employee's shoes and knows exactly what he or she is going through.

"It's just a very important part of our company philosophy and culture," Andy Taylor explains. "As people matriculate up through our system, they must never forget the importance of taking care of customers. They need to know how to run a branch on a busy day and learn what customer service is all about by delivering it. These are all skills you must have to be a part of management at any level in this company."

In addition to allowing for continuity and rewarding hard work, promoting from within creates a much more stable work environment and fosters teamwork instead of internal jealousies and competition. Employees know that someone from the outside won't suddenly come in and become their supervisor. Everyone at the top has been exactly where you are, and each employee's hard work will be rewarded with future promotions.

In fact, a manager can't succeed at Enterprise unless he or she makes others successful. Enterprise rigorously tracks the mentoring records of its managers, including whom they promoted and how those workers wind up doing in their new positions. This means that managers work hard to train everyone on their team and are continuously looking for opportunities to get high potential performers advanced through the system. The better these subordinates do, the better the manager looks—and the higher up he or she will advance in the system as well.

"When a great job opportunity comes along, as a manager you are looking for someone to promote," explains Doug Brown. "You say, 'Do I have a star for you!' Instead of hanging on to these people, you're out campaigning for them. And if they succeed, that's one more notch in your belt."

There's no better example of promoting from within and having managers work their way up than CEO Andy Taylor himself. When he got his driver's license at age sixteen, Enterprise was still primarily a local leasing company. "Dad was thrilled, because he put me right to work," Andy recalls. His first job: joining Jack on repo missions. Repossessions are an unavoidable part of auto sales and leasing, since inevitably some people fall behind on their payments.

During the summer of his sixteenth birthday, when he started working for his dad, Andy also did duty in the Lindburg Cadillac service department, delivering cars. When he was done at 5:00 P.M., he'd go see what Don Ross and Doug Brown were up to. Andy was sensitive about being the boss's son, determined to show he could succeed based on his own talent and hard work, and not just because of his lineage. After one mechanic took to calling him "the brave," a sarcastic reference to being the son of the company's chief, Andy took on the dirtiest, most challenging jobs he could find at the dealership and leasing office, eager to prove himself.

Andy began working at Enterprise full-time in 1973. By then he'd graduated from the University of Denver with a degree in business administration and had spent three years working as a general troubleshooter at a Lincoln-Mercury dealership and leasing company in San Francisco managed by Jack's brother, Paul. During this time, Andy got married to the former Barbara Broadhurst.

Set Realistic Expectations

Today, Enterprise receives about 300,000 résumés a year for its management-trainee program. When it comes to university graduates, the company prefers those with at least some prior work experience, preferably in a customer-oriented environment. Having been part of a sports team or other school activities is also a positive.

While the company tells candidates of the future potential rewards it offers, it makes sure to set proper expectations up front. No one is going to become a general manager overnight; advancement is a multiyear proposition.

"Most people aren't looking at 'Where am I going to retire?'—especially when they're just getting out of college," says chief operating officer Pam Nicholson. "They're looking at 'Where can I be in the next two years?' That's why it's very important for us to show them this is a company they can be with for a long time. But they need to understand what's realistic in the short term. We're careful about being up front with candidates about the opportunities. The last thing we want to do is overpromise. We'd rather people know exactly what to expect, and accept the job knowing what they're going to see or do as soon as they get here."

As a result, Enterprise has an impressive 70 percent retention rate for its full-time workforce.

"The highest turnover is really in the first year, where candidates discover whether this business is right for them," Nicholson says. "By the time they get to the branch manager level, they very rarely leave. By then, they get it and understand what we're all about. They know why they're here and can see that all of their work has been worth it. They start to feel that true ownership of running a business and how it's fun to make your own decisions and get paid on what you are doing."

What are the traits the most successful managers share in keeping employees over the long haul?

1. They hire only the best candidates, even when tempted to lower their standards during times of high employment.
2. They are very clear in explaining the job and expectations for advancement.
3. They communicate the company's mission and give examples of how it applies to what employees do every day.
4. They offer employees a "big picture look" after ninety days to solidify their views of what the company offers.
5. They make sure to use Enterprise's philosophy of "customers and employees first" as their guide.
6. They focus on employee training, development, and mentorship.
7. They explain the importance of starting at the bottom in the Enterprise management development system.
8. They celebrate and recognize every employee, branch, and group success, while making a big deal about promotions.
9. They are honest with workers and always let them know where they stand.

10. They listen to employees and show how the company has implemented and acted upon their feedback.
11. They lead by example and convey a positive message about where the company is going.
12. They never accept anything less than excellence.

Train Thoroughly

New management trainees are first assigned to a branch office. It's been called a "business boot camp" and been compared to an accelerated real-world MBA. Enterprise calls it an "MBA without the IOU." Some employees specifically come to work for the company just to go through this program, knowing that the skills gathered through it will be marketable elsewhere if, for any reason, they decide not to stay with Enterprise. Interestingly enough, the company hires very few degreed MBAs, because it likes to teach the fundamentals of running a business The Enterprise Way, rather than attempting to have candidates relearn what they've already been taught in school.

During this training program, which is done primarily at the branch level, trainees learn how to manage profit-and-loss reports, control expenses, and implement comprehensive business development and marketing plans. They also work behind the counter, learning what it takes to meet the needs of customers one-on-one.

Most branches now have people on hand to wash and prepare cars, but it's not unusual to find new recruits—or managers, for that matter—helping out if that's what's needed to get a car ready for a customer. Everyone is taught to do whatever it takes to assist and satisfy Enterprise customers. Performing what some see as grunt work can help to create a stronger bond among all team members—after all, everyone has been there. Management trainees also pick up customers, handle complaints, resolve problems, and make crucial decisions. Such an accelerated on-the-job learning approach gives everyone a feeling of confidence that the company believes in them and paves the way for increased responsibility down the road.

One of the key workshops all trainees attend is a class designed to teach them how to build exceptional customer relationships. They are also introduced to Enterprise's mission statement:

Our mission is to fulfill the automobile and commercial truck rental, leasing, car sales, and related needs of our customers and, in doing so, exceed their expectations for service, quality, and value.

We will strive to earn our customers' long-term loyalty by working to deliver more than promised, being honest and fair, and "going the extra mile" to provide exceptional personalized service that creates a pleasing business experience.

We must motivate our employees to provide exceptional service to our customers by supporting their development, providing opportunities for personal growth, and fairly compensating them for their successes and achievements.

We believe it is critical to our success to promote managers from within who will serve as examples of success for others to follow.

Although it is our goal to be the best and not necessarily the biggest or most profitable, our success at satisfying customers and motivating employees will bring growth and long-term profitability.

The trainee's study of customer service continues with a straightforward assignment: Think of a time when you felt that a company went out of its way to make you feel good about doing business with it. Next, figure out what the company did or said to make you feel this way. The answers are often very similar:

Employees welcomed me with a warm greeting; then they smiled, didn't rush me, followed up with phone calls, thanked me for my business, offered solutions for my problems, and further provided suggestions that might help me with my concerns.

Then trainees are asked to consider the flip side: Think of a time you did business with a company that made you feel you were *not* important. What did the company do or say to make you feel this way? Often, such reactions were the result of employees who were abrupt or rude, acted like the customer was inconveniencing them, or lied. In virtually all cases, the reasons generally have to do with something employees did or didn't do, as opposed to the product or service itself.

This exercise is designed to show trainees that the same is true at Enterprise: To the company's customers, Enterprise's branch employees are the organization. It is the small things Enterprise employees—the company's representatives—do each day that sustain Enterprise's image and cultivate its reputation. People can go to many businesses to rent a car. Customers choose Enterprise because of how they are treated.

To drive the point closer to home, Enterprise makes it clear that trainees are not just in the car rental business—they are in the people and relationship-building business. How do you build customer relationships? Enterprise advises its employees to use these twelve essential steps:

1. Acknowledge the customer's presence with a smile or handshake.
2. Be enthusiastic.
3. *Always* make eye contact.
4. Speak in a friendly manner.
5. If you know the customer's name (Mr., Mrs., last name), use it in your greeting. Since the company asks for identification,

there's no reason not to start using the customer's name right away. But it's important not to overuse one's name—the point is not to sound phony, but to be genuine. And never call an older person by their first name unless you have been asked to do so by the customer.

6. Listen actively and carefully without interrupting or allowing yourself to be distracted. Customers should be given your total attention.

7. Offer solutions. Don't *tell* the customer to do anything.

8. Provide unsolicited help (directions, maps, etc.).

9. Be positive in your comments, such as "We appreciate your business" and "Drive safely." Upon dropping the car off, always say, "Thank you and come see us again" and offer a handshake, if appropriate.

10. Remember: It's the customer's *perception* that counts.

11. Try to anticipate the needs of customers. Always "hurry" to help.

12. Never use industry slang or terminology. Instead, use everyday words that customers can clearly understand. And never talk down to a customer. Treat him or her as a valued guest.

EIGHT STEPS TO TURNING AN ANGRY CUSTOMER AROUND

No matter how conscientious and accommodating you are, at times you will find yourself dealing with an upset customer. Perhaps their vacation plans have been thrown into disarray, or they are upset about an accident that is the reason they need to a rent a car in the first place. At Enterprise, employees are taught to do the following in attempting to turn a volatile situation around:

1. Actively listen with an understanding attitude.
2. Record what the customer tells you.
3. Apologize.
4. Find out what the customer wants.
5. Propose a solution and attempt to get the customer's buy-in.
6. If the customer doesn't like your solution, ask them what a fair resolution would be.
7. Follow up by calling your customer to ensure their satisfaction.
8. Never let the customer lose face.

Hire "Customer-Focused" People

Although the basics of customer service can be taught to anyone, some people are better able to deal with the public than others. That's why Enterprise is so careful about whom it brings on board in the first place. To help pinpoint the best prospects, the company uses behavioral-based interviewing techniques, asking candidates to give examples of how they've helped people in the past, whether in a previous job or life in general, to illustrate their understanding of other people and the fundamentals of customer service.

By asking potential employees to recount examples of situations where they've dealt with difficult people in the past, or have gone above and beyond what is required to solve a problem or to deliver excellent service, Enterprise is able to identify the kind of candidates that will fit in best with its customer-centric viewpoint. The company looks for the following critical skills, which Enterprise has found are exhibited by those best able to consistently deliver excellent customer service:

1. A passion for taking care of customers.
2. A willingness to be flexible. (Taking care of customers isn't about reciting policy. It requires listening. Each situation is different; employees must share initiative in finding new ways to address the needs of every person.)
3. A work ethic based on dedication to the company and its mission.
4. An eagerness to learn a new business and work their way up.
5. Self-motivation and goal-orientation. (This is essential in a performance-driven environment like Enterprise's.)
6. Persuasive sales skills. (In addition to selling services to retail customers, employees are heavily involved in the business-to-business side of the operation. Strong sales skills will allow them to build relationships with other businesses and keep the company growing.)
7. Excellent communication skills.
8. Leadership ability. (This is particularly important, since all of the company's managers come from within the organization.)

Monitor Progress and Provide Regular Feedback

Mentoring is a key part of Enterprise's culture. By the end of their first year, employees are already helping to train new hires, even as they continue to learn the ins and outs of the business themselves. Teaching valuable skills to others helps to further your knowledge, Enterprise has found.

The success of an Enterprise branch requires strong business-to-business relationships. New employees are quickly trained in this part of the operation, calling on insurance agents, claims representatives, repair shops, car dealerships, and businesses with corporate accounts. Each new hire is given a territory along with specific targets or goals. They are responsible for finding new business and growing existing accounts in their territory. Setting milestones, with meaningful rewards and recognition, helps Enterprise keep new managers energized and committed.

"We almost re-recruit each day to make sure that once people are in the company they see the opportunities to stay with us and grow," says Enterprise president Don Ross.

One effective way to keep new hires focused is with regular reviews. At Enterprise, trainees are evaluated several times during their first year. It is a practice that dates back to the early 1980s, when the company was experiencing double-digit annual growth and had begun to heavily recruit college graduates in order to fuel its expansion. At the time, personnel reviews were an informal process. "We just sat around the campfire and swapped stories," one company veteran says.

When Enterprise realized it had to update and refine its evaluation methods, the company created a new model based on something new college recruits would be familiar with: quarterly grades.

"People who attain college degrees have been getting tests and quarterly grades for sixteen years," Doug Brown explains. "We had to challenge them the same way they've been challenged and recognized in school. We needed rapid development, evaluations, and advancement."

The performance benchmarks and definable goals that are a part of these evaluations mesh well with the academic review model. But they have other important benefits as well.

"If you make career paths and success more definable, it prevents people from saying, 'I didn't get promoted because they didn't like me,' or 'He got promoted because he's a cousin,'" Brown says.

For most new hires, primary training at Enterprise lasts about eight months. It concludes with a management qualification inter-view, also known as "the grill." In this sit-down oral exam, the management trainees face a regional or group manager who pep-pers them with questions about every aspect of the business. It can be a nerve-racking experience, and that's how it's intended. Man-agement wants to see how much the novices have learned and how well they handle pressure.

After successfully completing the initial training period, employees are promoted to management assistant and then assis-tant branch manager. As an assistant branch manager, they begin to receive a percentage of the branch's profits every month. That percentage increases with each promotion.

It is within the reach of a new management trainee to rise to the level of general manager. In fact, every Enterprise general manager began his or her career as a management trainee. Such high per-formers are among the top-paid individuals in the company.

It is at the assistant branch manager level that doors first begin to open wide for increased opportunities throughout the com-pany. In the job review and future goals forms managers period-ically submit, they are encouraged to write down their long-term career aspirations. The company does its best to help employees reach these objectives.

Within four to six years, motivated workers may be promoted to the position of area manager, responsible for three or four branches and sharing in the profits of each branch. But one's career path at Enterprise doesn't necessarily lead straight up. Along the way, managers may have to take a step backward to get ahead. A branch manager might build up a location, make it highly profitable, and then be asked to move to a poorly per-forming branch or a new office to work the same magic once again. Or a regional vice president, who's overseeing several area managers, may be asked to relocate to a newer region with high potential to help grow the business. Since pay is tied to profits, they might not see an increase in compensation until their new operation starts to hit on all cylinders. But such employees recognize that there may be greater opportunity and future earnings potential for those who succeed at each step along the way, as well as those willing to help the company when needed.

Offer Alternative Career Paths

Not every management trainee ultimately chooses a rental management career path. Along the way they might develop a greater interest in recruiting, remarketing, car sales, fleet services, or finance. In such cases, they can move ahead at Enterprise by following in a slightly different path. The company's operating divisions have localized departments in a variety of areas.

Giving workers the chance to move around within different divisions of the company benefits both employees and the overall organization. Employees are able to expand their horizons, learn new skills, and work in areas they enjoy. Enterprise, in turn, retains quality people who are well versed in the company's culture and customer service ethos.

Diversify Your Workforce

Workplace diversity—assuring equal opportunities regardless of race, gender, age, or sexual orientation—is a key issue within Enterprise and the business world at large. Legal statutes and multimillion-dollar judgments against non-compliant companies have drawn the attention of corporate America. Nevertheless, according to a study by the National Urban League (which was

funded by Enterprise Rent-A-Car), only about one in three workers believe their employer is doing enough to foster workplace
diversity.

Enterprise, like a growing number of employers, sees diversity
as an advantage. That view is backed up by research. A study of
Fortune 500 companies by the University of Texas at the Dallas
School of Management found that workplace diversity has a
positive impact on the bottom line of companies that rely on team
structures, have aggressive growth strategies, and operate in
fluid markets—a spot-on description of Enterprise's business
environment.

Diversity helps organizational performance because it brings in
a multiplicity of ideas and approaches to achieving goals and dealing with problems. In service businesses, a diverse workforce
makes it more likely that the team will be able to recognize and
respond to the needs of a varied customer base. Not surprisingly,
customers are typically more comfortable dealing with someone
they can relate to and who reflects their same background.

Capitalizing on the potential benefits of diversity takes commitment. At Enterprise, a corporate diversity manager, assistant vice
president, and vice president of corporate relations work with
the senior vice president of human resources to coordinate the
company's overall diversity strategy. The objective is to create a
workforce in every market that mirrors the diversity of the local
community.

"We don't set quotas," says Ross. "We say, 'Reflect your local
market.' We want people who speak the same language, literally
and figuratively, as our customers."

Each operating group establishes diversity goals based on the
demographics of that market. For example, if an area has a large
Hispanic population, Enterprise works hard to hire and develop

a relatively high percentage of Hispanic managers. In fact, managers are evaluated and rewarded based on how successful they are at hiring and developing employees that reflect their local markets. Companywide, about 35 percent of Enterprise's new recruits are members of a minority group; some 40 percent of the full-time workforce are women.

When Enterprise began as a leasing company, the salesmen Jack Taylor hired were white males, but so were many of his customers. Back then it was almost unheard of to find women in the auto industry. Not so today.

"We're definitely conscious of opening our doors and expanding our workforce," Pam Nicholson insists. "It's not like the early days, when companies hired one type of person. But we do look for common traits in all of our people: hard work and entrepreneurship. That's what breeds success." And Enterprise's team of recruiters reflects this attitude. Among them are men and women of all colors, nationalities, and ages—similar to the broad mix of candidates the company is looking to hire.

THE ENTERPRISE WAY

1. Hire smart people and train them in your practices from the ground up.
2. Allow employees to work their way up, and make a commitment to reward their efforts by promoting from within.
3. When hiring someone new, set realistic expectations about what type of compensation they can look forward to receiving now and over the next several years. That way, no one is disappointed down the line.

4. Clearly communicate the company's mission from day one.

5. Continuously train employees about your business and on the best ways to take care of customers.

6. Provide regular performance reviews—several times during year one and at least annually thereafter—to give employees regular feedback.

7. To deliver excellent customer service, hire "customer-focused" people. Put together a series of behavioral-based questions during the interview process that encourage applicants to demonstrate how they have taken care of customers in the past.

8. In order to take good care of your customers, employees must have a willingness to be flexible, a dedicated work ethic, eagerness to learn the business, solid communication skills, and strong leadership abilities.

9. Help employees set long-term goals, then regularly follow up to make sure they are on track to meet these objectives.

10. Allow talented workers to move into other areas of the business if they show a desire to do so and have the right skill sets for the position.

11. Maintain a highly diversified workforce and recruitment team that accurately reflects the world at large and the customers you serve each day.

Treat Everyone
Like an Owner

USINESS OWNERS CARE more about the performance and longevity of their company than anyone else. After all, their livelihoods, reputations, and futures depend on the operation's success. Since owners are compensated based on the bottom line, they have an incentive to continually come up with new and better ways of doing things, different methods for satisfying and finding new customers, and innovative techniques for cutting costs in practical ways. It's therefore no surprise that many corporations use a variety of techniques to make employees feel more like "owners."

Some award stock options, which presumably become more valuable as the company's financial results improve, thus giving employees an economic incentive to make the business more prosperous. Others offer workers the option to buy company stock at a discount and/or offer annual bonuses based on both the individual's and the corporation's overall performance.

But few do as much as Enterprise to truly allow employees to behave like and be compensated as owners. This feeling of entrepreneurship spurs everyone at the company to perform at their highest potential every day. And while the approach and incentives

Enterprise uses might appear to be more costly than necessary on the surface, the company's innovative pay-for-performance plan is really what has made it so successful for such a long time.

In this chapter, we'll explore Enterprise's unique operational structure as well as its generous compensation program. Indeed, Enterprise pays out almost 40 percent of all company profits to employees.

Decentralize Operations

Enterprise is akin to a franchise operation in the way it has structured its global business, with one headquarters at the top and hundreds of small self-run businesses below. While corporate headquarters in St. Louis provides full support and general guidance for all of the company's nearly 7,000 locations, each branch runs its own operations under the direction of a general manager. The general managers, in turn, report back to a senior vice president at the corporate office, who serves primarily as a liaison between local groups and headquarters. Unlike a traditional franchise, however, the employees charged with operating each of these branches are not required to put up any kind of upfront investment. Like a franchise, however, the "owner-operators" are paid based on the profitability of their individual units.

"I like to think of all of these groups as subsidiaries of the parent," says chief operating officer Pam Nicholson. "As we continue to grow, we break our operations into new groups. Even though we're a big company, we like to run it as a small business, giving managers the autonomy to make decisions that are close to home."

"I call it a collection of entrepreneurial businesses where everyone has ownership and a say in how things are done," adds CEO Andy Taylor.

Enterprise's operating structure consists of groups, regions, areas, and branches and works something like this:

The "group" is managed by a general manager, who oversees the "region," "areas," and "branches" underneath. Each group is like a mini division of the entire company, with its own rental, human resources, accounting, and remarketing operations. Depending on the group, it may also run other Enterprise businesses, such as fleet services, retail used-car sales, and commercial truck rentals. If a group is large enough to be regionalized, each region is run by a regional vice president who has direct responsibility for managing the various areas and branches. Every area is overseen by an area manager whom the managers of each branch report to.

While the specific group, region, area, and branch structure vary depending on the geographic location and size of the rental fleet in various parts of the world, this overall organizational concept always remains the same.

"There are usually six or seven area managers within a group," president Don Ross explains. "Normally, three to five branches report to each area manager."

Southern California, for instance, is part of what's known as "Group 32." Within Group 32 are 13 regions, with 6,500 employees and dozens of areas and hundreds of branches underneath. While the branches make many of their own decisions, they are supported by the resources of Group 32 headquarters in Gardena, outside of Los Angeles. At the same time, they can draw upon the resources of the corporate office in St. Louis for everything from marketing materials to technology support. There are nearly 80 operating groups and 150 regions companywide.

"Employees run each of these groups and branches as individual businesses," says Nicholson. "Everything is done locally. Each group has its own accounting, recruitment, car sales, and marketing teams. They really are self-sufficient operations."

The groups, regions, areas, and branches operate autonomously, because Enterprise believes it knows what's best for its specific community and customer base.

"Culturally, when building a large company, you have two approaches," says one of the company's early general managers. "First, you can take an approach where you standardize everything and manage by policy. In this case, you own the brand but not the heart of the operation. That's mostly what you see in the business world today. By contrast, you can attempt to build the equivalent of a franchise operation in terms of how a corporation looks vis-à-vis its branches, people, and cities and treat these people like owners—allowing them to function in the spirit of entrepreneurship. That's a whole different method of management. And it's what Enterprise is all about."

A few areas of the business are coordinated at the national level, such as marketing and corporate communications, to ensure that the brand is consistently presented across the organization. Otherwise, the groups are allowed to operate independently, down to managing their own profit-and-loss statements.

"The general manager of each group has his or her own business functions and pulls and manages all of his or her own financial information," Ross says. "This information is then sent to the corporate office, where we audit it. In some cases, these folks are running operations that generate hundreds of millions in revenue each year."

One factor involved in whether someone is promoted further up the ladder is how well they manage the income and balance sheet. But this audit process isn't just a matter of big brother looking over the operator's shoulder.

"We use this to show each branch how their costs and revenues compare to other branches each month," says Nicholson. "We are then able to show them where their fleet mixes might be out of balance and help them to improve operations in ways that lead to increased revenues."

Sharing this information allows managers to better understand what their costs, receivables, and bad debts look like. It also helps them figure out whether to add or remove certain cars from the fleet, and when the right time is to start putting some of the vehicles up for resale.

Although headquarters negotiates pricing and purchasing terms for the entire company's worldwide fleet, the buy is based on orders placed by the individual groups. Each group sends in specific requests from a list of available vehicles and manufacturers that Enterprise does business with. The final corporate buy is influenced by what the branches feel will be the most in-demand vehicles at their specific location in the coming twelve months. Negotiating the deal corporately brings the per-car price down, though money to pay for the vehicles comes out of the budgets of each individual operating group and the cars are ultimately purchased from local dealers.

"Each one of our operations places their order at the beginning of the year," says Nicholson. "If it's a 10,000-car operation, they might say, 'I need 10,000 total cars. Of that, give me 3,000 economy cars, 2,000 midsized cars, 500 SUVs, 300 luxury vehicles, and so forth.' We take all these orders, put them together, and then go to the manufacturers on their behalf to negotiate a buy of 600,000 or so total vehicles."

The groups also decide what additional business units to start (such as fleet services, car sales, and truck rentals) and whom to hire and fire. They often make decisions about real estate purchases, although headquarters maintains a special department to support and oversee such efforts.

Enterprise actually has a very small headquarters, considering the size of the company. About 2,000 people work at its St. Louis corporate campus; more than half of those are part of the technology team. "The functions we focus on at headquarters are information technology, treasury, insurance, legal, and legislative issues," Ross says. "We also have marketing and communications departments and national marketing teams to work with the insurance companies on a corporate level. But very little of what we do is centralized to headquarters."

"I regard our headquarters as a massive switching station of ideas," Andy Taylor says. "At most companies, people are always looking up on high and asking, 'What do you want me to do?' We take another path. We look to our people and say, 'Do the right thing for your customers and your teams.' We let them figure it out."

Pay Workers Well

As previously noted, employees reaching the assistant manager level begin to receive both a base salary and a cut of the profits from the business.

"This gives even the greenest of managers a feeling of ownership," Nicholson says. "They're paid on the branch, and they are promoted based on the performance of that branch. It really is about creating opportunities for employees. They know that if they do the right things, first and foremost taking care of our customers, they'll be rewarded."

Jack Taylor first got a taste of what it was like to be an owner when running his small package delivery business. He also saw the benefits as an employee at Lindburg Cadillac, where he received a base salary and 15 percent cut of the profits from all the sales he brought in. When he founded Enterprise, Jack wanted to give his own employees a similar compensation plan and the same feeling of ownership. He wanted them to share in the company's success. Nothing, he realized, would motivate them more.

"If I give someone a piece of the action or a bonus based on profits, they are going to do a better job every time," he says. As Andy Taylor adds, "It means you'll get dinged when you have a bad debt or too many expenses, but you'll do well as you get new customers and old ones return."

While most companies see the payroll as a drag on the bottom line, Enterprise has always thrived on spreading the wealth. Much of that has to do with Jack's logic about why paying good people more money is beneficial to the company.

"Let's say you make $100,000 for the business and I give you 10 percent of that as a bonus, or $10,000," he offers. "By that logic, if you make us $1 million, you get $100,000. Would I rather have you make the extra $10,000 or $100,000? It's obvious. I'd much rather pay you $100,000. The more you make, the more the business makes. Why wouldn't I want that to happen?"

There was a more pragmatic side to the company's generous compensation structure in the company's early days as well. Jack worried about the financial drain guaranteed salaries would have in slow times, and he hated the thought of ever laying anyone off. As someone who was always cautious about growth and managing risk, Jack decided to promise employees more on the back end in lieu of providing a higher base salary up front. His strategy also helped to attract and motivate the sort of people he was looking to hire: those with an entrepreneurial mind-set willing to place part of their salary at risk in exchange for a huge potential upside.

Because of Enterprise's pay structure, some longtime company executives now enjoy significant pay packages. "Some people in the company make more than $1 million a year," Jack says proudly. "Does it bother me that we're paying them so much? No. I think it's wonderful, because in order for them to get that $1 million, if they are on a 10 percent bonus plan, they've got to be generating $10 million for the business."

A Deal Is a Deal

It would be easy to change its compensation structure now that Enterprise is so successful. The company is free to alter the rules, or simply cut out the profit component altogether, especially for its highest-earning managers. But Jack and Andy Taylor insist that won't happen on their watches.

"We believe a deal is a deal," Andy Taylor says. "You're helping us drive this success. Therefore, we're going to compensate you like we said we would five or ten years ago, on that same percentage."

Knowing the company's word is good is a crucial component to giving employees a sense of ownership. If they feel the rules will change after they've worked so hard to bring business into your company, they are less likely to do so in the first place. Enterprise wants its people to be ambitious and confident without feeling like someone is always looking over their shoulders or about to change how the game is played.

Back in the 1950s, Jack got to know many high-earning salesmen who worked for a national dressmaking company headquartered near Lindburg Cadillac. "Every time one of them started making too much money, the company would split his territory to cut it down, without paying residuals on business that had already been brought in," Jack recalls. "Not surprisingly, the salesmen would get really mad. When their pay was cut, they'd leave and go work for another company. This hurt the dressmaker in the long run, and it's one of the reasons I decided to do things differently."

"If a person is making a lot of money here, he or she is doing something really right," Andy Taylor adds. "As long as they stay humble and continue to treat our customers and employees well, why wouldn't I want to keep that person with us, instead of hiring someone else for less who might not be as effective? At the end of the day, we're all going to benefit. It's fantastic that some of our people make so much money. It means we're all successful."

Pay on Company and Individual Performance

Enterprise not only pays its people a percentage of profits from their individual branches, but as they are promoted to the area, region, and ultimately the group level, they receive a share of profits from all of the operating units underneath them. Not surprisingly, these sums can really add up. That's why everyone is so focused on moving up the ladder at Enterprise. Each promotion leads to a higher paycheck, as well as more responsibility to make a difference and lead change within the organization.

In another break with convention, Enterprise pays bonuses on a monthly basis (instead of annually), based on the profitability of the company that month. As a result, paychecks vary from period to period. Employees start out with a target annual compensation amount, which represents an estimate of how much they will make during the year between their base salary and anticipated monthly bonuses. Employees are then left to budget their monthly expenses accordingly, knowing that June's paycheck is bound to be higher than the one they receive in the short rental month of February.

"We had some challenging years back when our overall operating costs were higher than they should have been, and profits fell slightly because of that," Ross admits. "This meant that a lot of people made less than they did the year before. But that's the way it works. When you have a compensation structure like this, it can go both ways, although that has rarely been the case at Enterprise."

Employees of the various group-level support departments (such as recruitment and marketing), as well as other divisions of the operation (remarketing and fleet sales), also receive a bonus paid based upon the bottom line of the group and division they work for.

Employees at corporate headquarters in such areas as information technology and corporate communications who support the entire operation are often offered a choice: They can either receive a set salary, or take a slightly lower base and receive a percentage of profits from the entire organization.

"There's no such thing as our people making too much money in our book," adds Doug Brown. "Employees making lots of money are legend at Enterprise because of our structure, but the company's own profitability has grown in line with this. It's funny, because when I was active in the business, graduates at places like Emory or New York University would say, 'Why should I go to work for a rental car company?' We'd tell them that if they stuck it out, in four or five years they'd be making a lot more than any of their classmates."

Once employees begin to be paid off a portion of the profits (from assistant branch managers on up to CEO Andy Taylor), their base salary is between $25,000 and $35,000 a year. But the amount of compensation tied to performance can be substantial. While a branch manager might have only 10 percent or 20 percent of his or her salary at risk in the form of a bonus, 80 percent or more of a general manager's overall compensation comes from profitability. For some corporate officers, that number can be as high as 99 percent.

Corporate and senior vice presidents have their incentive pay split: 75 percent comes from how the operating units under them perform, with the remaining 25 percent based on the performance of the overall corporation. "We want them to have a balanced view, so they do what's right for the entire company, not just for the groups they manage," Ross says.

In all cases, the percentage of profits each employee receives is made clear up front, so there are never any surprises or misunderstandings. It changes only when someone is promoted.

"In most companies, nobody cares if the lights are on, because they're not paying the light bills," observes Brown. "There isn't a single Enterprise branch where the manager isn't worried about whether lights are on that shouldn't be because the money to pay the electricity bill is coming directly out of their paycheck."

One risk of tying compensation in with the profit-and-loss statement is that it has the potential to encourage short-term thinking and cause one to cut corners at the expense of customer service. Enterprise keeps this in check by tying promotions in with delivering good customer service. In fact, the only way to move up at Enterprise is by wowing the company's customers. Those who scrimp in ways that detract from the customer experience quickly learn this is a penny-wise, pound-foolish approach.

Ownership Improves Operational Efficiencies

Providing a sense of ownership to those in the field has many advantages when it comes to implementing operational plans. Handing out edicts from above that everyone is forced to blindly follow can backfire. That's why Enterprise usually tends to go with the ideas generated from its branches, even when executives are convinced that corporate's way is better.

Enterprise's ownership structure gives employees the freedom to try new things—and make mistakes. At many companies, employees often feel their jobs may be in jeopardy if they try something new that fails to take off as expected. Enterprise executives realize that mistakes lead to opportunities. Employees are encouraged to continually try new things, even at the risk of what may be perceived to be failure. Enterprise has found that, in reality, most decisions an individual employee makes will cost you little more than a bit of money if they're wrong. Giving them the freedom to take risks contributes to this environment of high performance, accountability, and ownership the company is trying to instill. "You just don't want to make anyone accountable by telling them their jobs are on the line for taking these risks," Andy Taylor says. "If you do that, they'll never try anything new. Taking risk is part and parcel of being successful."

It's through taking risks that new ideas are discovered, leading to more efficient operations and benefiting every branch in the process. "If a certain operating group comes to us and says they've found a better way to make a cheeseburger, so to speak, we'll ask for a taste of it," Andy Taylor says. "If it's good, we'll take it to other places and test it further. If it works, and we are able to roll it out across the system, the results can be amazing."

This is in line with Andy Taylor's desire to keep every branch in "balance" in four core areas: growth, profitability, customer service, and employee development. When any one area is out of kilter, it has a tendency to immediately drift down to the bottom line. That's why, in addition to getting help and support at the corporate level, branches and groups turn to other branches and groups throughout the organization to share ways of continually improving operations across the various business units.

Incentive Pay Increases Retention

Instilling a sense of ownership helps the company in its recruitment and retention efforts as well. The company's entrepreneurial culture and the enthusiasm it generates make current employees one of Enterprise's best sources of new recruits. Fully 40 percent of all new hires come from employee referrals.

"They tell their friends and families about us," Nicholson says. "Our satisfied customers do the same thing. They tell others about us, they come back, and they bring us new businesses partners, all of which helps each branch to grow. This, in turn, allows us to open new locations and promote people as the region gets larger. And it all happens because our employees have ownership. They're not only paid on today's profitability, but they know that taking care of customers will generate growth, and therefore a bigger paycheck."

And that is what leads to higher retention. "If you are successful at Enterprise, you will be paid more than the competition could ever think about giving you," Andy Taylor maintains. "I remember a while back the CEO of another rent-a-car company was playing golf with a banker friend of mine. He told the banker, 'Did you know that Enterprise pays some of its people more than $1 million a year?' The man at the car rental company was in absolute shock that we would do this."

Family Businesses Can Work Well

Enterprise today is owned almost entirely by the Taylor family.

"We had some stock out there for a while owned by what I refer to as the pioneers of the company, those Jack gave equity to in the early days," Andy Taylor says. "As the company got bigger after I became president in the 1980s, I changed the structure a bit because we had all of these different subsidiaries that general managers had stock in, and it was becoming a problem. We ultimately decided to roll everything up into the parent company."

Enterprise has been closely controlled by the Taylor family ever since. They have opted to finance future growth through profits and corporate financing, rather than by going public and becoming subject to the whims of shareholders and Wall Street.

The company has become a role model for how to effectively preserve a family-owned business. Such businesses generate half of the gross domestic product in the United States, hire 60 percent of American workers, and create 78 percent of all new jobs, according to a recent study by the University of Southern Maine's institute for family business. Yet only one out of every three family businesses survives into the second generation. Personal conflicts can frequently impinge on prudent business considerations and decisions.

That makes Enterprise's track record all the more remarkable. When Jack began to transition some of his leadership responsibilities in 1980, when Andy was named president, the company was already more than 20 years old. That year, Enterprise had revenues of just over $78 million and fewer than 200 employees. By 2006, revenues had jumped to nearly $9 billion.

Jack gradually turned management control of the company over to Andy during the course of several years. Starting with Andy's rise to president in 1980, he was promoted again in 1991 to chief executive officer, at which point he was leading all aspects of the company. In a symbolic gesture, he also assumed the title of chairman in 2001. Jack believes that keeping Enterprise a privately owned, family-run business is what has allowed it to prosper all this time.

"If it weren't for Andy agreeing to take over, I probably would have sold the company," Jack admits. "Occasionally, my ego gets a little insecure and I'll wonder why Andy didn't call me before making certain decisions. But that's part of the challenge in giving up a business that you've built like this. It's tough. A lot of people can't do it. Fortunately, I was able to, and it's why we've been able to expand and get as big as we are."

It is also one reason Jack decided to stay in his old office at the company's original headquarters instead of moving to the company's modern, larger corporate campus down the street—he wanted to stay out of Andy's way.

"I decided in 1991 if I was going to make Andy CEO, I couldn't be around trying to second-guess him, or having other executives run in to ask me what I thought all the time," Jack says. "That's what would happen if I had an office next door or down the hall from Andy. The separation is important. It makes the lines clearer as to who is in charge."

Today, a third generation of Taylors is working at the company. Andy's daughter, Christine (Chrissy), works as a corporate rental manager in Europe, while Jo Ann's daughter, Carolyn Kindle Payne, is a corporate rental manager based at corporate headquarters. After graduating from college, Chrissy and Carolyn both began as management trainees and are continuing to work their way up the system. Although a succession plan is in place, it will be up to them to decide how high up in the organization they want to go.

"We as a family have agreed that we want the company to remain privately owned by the Taylor family, with all generations involved in managing it," Carolyn says. "This gives us a huge competitive advantage. We don't have outside shareholders and are therefore able to operate Enterprise in the best way we see fit."

Even those family members not working for Enterprise on a day-to-day basis are involved in high-level meetings about its ongoing operation. The entire Taylor family, including those who don't work for the company, meets at least four times a year to discuss the business.

"One reason Enterprise works so well as a family business is because Andy, Jack, and my aunt have seen other family-owned businesses implode firsthand and they learned from that," Chrissy adds. "They've taken steps to make sure this doesn't happen here. Everyone does a good job of keeping the family close and preparing us for what may be coming down the road."

At the same time, non–family members continue to move up the ranks, with little worry the company will change its generous ownership-centered structure, which rewards them financially for excellent performance.

THE ENTERPRISE WAY

1. Set up a financial structure that gives employees a clear incentive to see the company grow and prosper.
2. As your company becomes bigger, allow local operations to function as highly independent "subsidiaries" while offering support at a corporate level. This gives employees a personal stake in ensuring that the operation succeeds.
3. Provide workers with the freedom to operate autonomously and make their own decisions.
4. While delegating more freedom to various business units, manage marketing and corporate communications at a corporate level to maintain a consistent message and brand.

5. Base promotions on how well individual employees are able to manage all aspects of the business under their control, including the profit-and-loss statement.

6. Share in the wealth, paying part of the company's profits out to employees across all parts of the organization on a regular basis, based on their responsibilities and the contributions they make to the business. Just make it clear what percentage they will receive so there are no surprises or disappointments when bonuses are handed out.

7. Once you strike a deal with employees, don't break it for any reason.

8. In a well-structured pay-for-performance system, revel in paying big bonuses to workers. It's an indication that your company is earning more money.

9. As employees take on more management responsibilities, allow them to earn a piece of the profits from each business unit they are in charge of running.

10. Encourage everyone to take risks—without the fear of being fired if things don't work out. Some of the best new discoveries come through taking chances and trying new things.

11. You don't have to hand out company stock to keep employees in the fold and make them perform like business owners, but you must be willing to share part of the wealth they are helping you create.

6

Form Strong Partnerships

BRIAN PASSELL SITS in the foyer of his office outside of Cleveland, Ohio, his jovial face and thick blond hair illuminated by two bright lights. After being dabbed with a bit of makeup to better enhance his features, he is checked by an assistant to see that his purple-and-black-striped tie is straight. Following a quick mike check, tape is rolled and Passell begins to speak.

"No matter what city you go to, there's going to be one very consistent experience, and that is you're going to have a bright, intelligent, hardworking, friendly person that's going to take care of that rental for you in a way that you just don't get with other rental car companies," he says. Passell, of course, is referring to Enterprise. While he knows the job at hand is to discuss some of the company's finer points, his comments are totally unscripted and completely off the cuff.

Before calling it a day, Passell trains his deep-blue eyes on the camera, intent on speaking directly to the Enterprise rental managers who will soon be watching this video: "Keep your promises every day of the week, even when they're tough to keep," he admonishes them. "Keep giving us the feedback so we can keep our part of the process right. And mostly I just want to say thank you for making a deal that seemed monumentally difficult to pull off exceed our expectations."

What might surprise you is that Passell doesn't work for Enterprise. He's not a director of the company, nor does he have any direct financial interest in its success. Rather, Passell is a top executive with Progressive, the third-largest auto insurer in the country, behind State Farm and Allstate. Although Progressive has been renting cars from Enterprise for decades, it only recently formalized a preferred-provider option agreement with the company, giving it special rates based on volume targets. This is one of dozens of similar agreements Enterprise has with insurance providers around the world. Because of these partnerships, Enterprise has become the leading car rental company that insurers send policyholders to first when they are in need of a replacement vehicle.

While it's unusual to see an executive from one company go on camera to sing the praises of another, it speaks to the hard-earned relationship Enterprise has with its many business partners—including insurers, auto manufacturers, corporations, car dealerships, body shops, and even credit unions. These partnerships have long been a key driver to the company's growth, and they give Enterprise an incredible competitive advantage. What might surprise you is how far the company goes to make these partnerships work—even if it means taking a temporary cut in business to ensure a win-win relationship for both sides.

It's All About Building Relationships

Enterprise began forming close partnerships with other businesses on day one. One of its first was with General Motors, which provided Cadillacs and other cars for the leasing operation.

"Jack's desire to develop deep business relationships with his partners goes way back," Andy Taylor observes. "For years, he used the same company to insure both his fleet and property. When his premium went up one year, instead of immediately looking for a lower price, he said, 'I'm not going to leave this insurance company to save a little money, because they treated me well for so long and I know I'll have coverage when times are tough and others can't get it.' At the same time, GMAC and the banks have long been loyal to him. It wasn't about getting the lowest rate and jumping around. It was about the relationship and knowing they offered stability, reliability, and took good care of us. We bring this same commitment to our many business partners today."

Enterprise's most crucial partnerships are those with the array of insurance providers, like Progressive, that send so much business its way. State Farm alone reserves an Enterprise car an average of once every nine seconds each business day. Enterprise's relationship with insurance companies dates back to the mid-1960s, when the three-man rental team of Don Ross, Wayne Kaufman, and Don Holtzman first convinced an adjuster to give the company a try. This has since grown to become a dominant part of Enterprise's business, accounting for more than half of all rental revenues. While other rental car companies covet this market and continually try to wrest market share away, Enterprise remains the preeminent leader in the insurance replacement rental field for several reasons.

For starters, Enterprise has worked hard to develop and maintain relationships with the insurance industry. Like so much else at the company, these relationships were initially built at the local level. Branch managers knocked on doors, frequently with a welcoming box of doughnuts in hand, to talk with adjusters and other insurance executives about the benefits of doing business with Enterprise. Why doughnuts? Because when business prospects associate you with something good, they are more likely to look forward to your sales call. These so-called doughnut runs were timed to arrive at insurance offices (as well as body shops and car dealerships) just as people were having their morning coffee. After exchanging pastries and pleasantries, Enterprise staffers would remind them that their branch was nearby and ready to help out when needed.

The breakfast treats were nice and always well received, but it was more about the conversations that went along with those doughnuts. For Enterprise, it was really about talking and listening to its customers—hearing their problems and concerns, and helping them to come up with solutions.

"In the early days, it also allowed us to drop off our bill and maybe pick up another rental deal," Ross recalls.

Beyond doughnuts, Enterprise managers have shown great creativity in embroidering the same general "get the word out" concept over the years, sometimes substituting such feel-good items as homemade brownies and cookies. During an oppressive summer heat wave, one manager even rented an ice cream truck and delivered refreshing treats on his run. In turn, prospects actually started smiling when Enterprise people came through the door—and looked forward to return visits.

These good gestures led to increased business and the creation of new services targeted at keeping these insurance companies—and their policyholders—happy. Enterprise's trademark "We'll Pick You Up" service began, in large part, as a way of convincing one insurance agent to rent replacement vehicles from the company.

As its insurance business grew, Enterprise branches started to do more to strengthen these partnerships. Among other things, Enterprise employees began offering to monitor a policyholder's entire repair process for the insurance company. Keep in mind that arranging for a replacement vehicle after an accident is much more complicated than renting a car from the airport. Since no one plans on having an accident, the need for a car often comes up quickly and unexpectedly. Many rentals are covered by insurance, but policies differ in terms of what they'll pay for, which can limit your options. Plus, when repairs are involved, the length of the rental is always in a state of flux. So, while you think you'll need the car for three or four days, it might actually wind up being a bit shorter or much longer, depending on how long it takes to complete the repair to your satisfaction.

Approval for the initial rental period is normally determined by the body shop's estimate of the repair completion date. If the work isn't finished on time, the rental must be extended by the adjuster to guarantee coverage. That's why Enterprise started following up with body shops from the moment a customer picked up their car, keeping the renter and insurance company in the loop about when these repairs would be finished. Enterprise then extended the length of the rental as necessary, normally after first reporting back to adjusters on the status and obtaining permission to do so. While this was a labor-intensive endeavor, it served to fulfill Enterprise's mission of providing superior service to both its own customers and its partner insurance companies.

For a long time, this whole process, including the final billing, was done manually. Enterprise employees often organized rental agreements in accordion files marked A, B, and C. A files were for the insurance companies, B files had records for the body and repair shops, and C files contained information on the renters. Under the original system, at times it took many phone calls, including some back-and-forth with the insurance company, to set up the rental in the first place, followed by conversations with policyholders to get things started. Then the process of checking on repairs, updating adjusters and customers, and getting approvals for any needed extensions could easily tack on another dozen calls. By the early 1990s, as the number of insurance rentals rapidly expanded, Enterprise's telephone traffic to handle this business systemwide shot up to the equivalent of 600,000 calls a day.

Create Greater Efficiencies

In 1994, Safeco, State Farm, and other insurers began talking with Enterprise about ways to cut down on the number of phone calls and faxes required to make a reservation by setting up some sort of national solution. Enterprise enlisted a trio of executives to work on developing a more practical and comprehensive automated program for taking care of the company's expanding roster of insurance customers, while making the rental process more efficient from all sides.

The team convened focus groups composed of claims adjusters and information services personnel from various insurance companies. Enterprise also held focus groups with its own people. In both cases, they charted the rental process from accident to repair completion and the eventual return of the vehicle. The Enterprise team then traveled to every region of the nation, visiting Geico offices to get an up-close look at the process in motion at the nation's third-largest auto insurer. At the first stop, a claims center in Virginia Beach, the team was stunned by the sheer volume of calls going to and coming from Enterprise branches—conversations that would monopolize the adjusters' day. Nearly all calls between the two companies were about extending customer rentals. The file loads and volume of electronic and phone traffic were astonishing. That's when Enterprise realized it had to find a way to make doing business with its insurance partners easier and more efficient.

Complicating this task was the complexity and diversity of the hardware and software systems used by the various insurance companies. Integrating new systems is never easy, and at times it's tough to get the people involved to embrace the needed changes. The solution, therefore, had to be flexible enough to work for everyone.

Enterprise set out to build what has come to be known as ARMS, short for Automated Rental Management System. The earliest iteration linked the insurance companies' mainframes to Enterprise's IBM AS/400 minicomputers. At its heart, the system was designed to let insurance companies manage the entire rental process with Enterprise electronically. Future versions would add to this experience by tracking the vehicle-repair process. This would create far greater efficiencies throughout the repair, reduce friction, and, frankly, lower the number of bothersome follow-up calls to all parties involved, including the insurance adjuster and repair shops.

The system, built to be as user-friendly as possible, works something like this: When a policyholder gets into an accident and files a claim, the insurance adjuster can log on to ARMS and create a reservation for the customer. This is electronically submitted to the appropriate Enterprise branch office, based on the customer's phone number or ZIP code, eliminating any calls or paperwork from the home office. Once the reservation is received, an Enterprise employee contacts the customer to set up the details of the rental, then monitors the whole process online. That way, adjusters can see how long the car is out while reading notes about what is happening along the way.

Without doing a cost analysis, Enterprise green-lighted development of the program, which wound up requiring an investment of around $40 million. Ironically, one of the main goals of the system was to give insurance companies a way to *reduce* the number of days cars are on rent by making the process as efficient as possible.

Not surprisingly, this commitment created resistance among some Enterprise field managers. Replacement vehicles, after all, are one of the key forces behind the company's ongoing growth. In 2000, the average replacement rental length was fourteen days. By the company's calculations, each day the average rental is reduced cuts the need for Enterprise's fleet down by 4 percent. This goes against its goal of growing the company by creating new opportunities for employees. If fewer rentals are necessary, this would stall growth—or at least that's what some thought.

A vocal group of senior field managers was furious. They balked at spending all that money for a program that would reduce earnings. A common refrain was "We're always saying the way you grow is by getting more cars. All of a sudden, we're coming up with a way to reduce rental days. This doesn't make sense."

But Enterprise determined that, if done correctly, ARMS would actually lead to *more* business, given the efficiencies it brought to the insurance companies and how happy that would make them.

"The decision to build ARMS was a slam dunk, because if you understand our culture and what we're all about, it comes down to doing the right thing," says Andy Taylor. "We're very decentralized, but we have a unique ability to rally around causes that are the right thing to do for our company and our business partners."

Train Thoroughly

Still, claims adjusters had to learn how to use ARMS before it could be fully embraced. In response, Enterprise set up a comprehensive training program. Adjusters from a few major insurance companies came to St. Louis to try out the pilot program and go through the modules on a prototype of the system. They were asked what could be improved and what they'd like to see. The adjusters were enthusiastic. But how, they asked, would their people around the country learn to use the system?

In response, Enterprise recruited some of its field managers to be system mentors. They were brought to headquarters to learn how to use ARMS, then flown around the country to train insurance company personnel. Several insurance companies asked Enterprise to station employees full-time at the claims center to help manage the process.

"At first people thought we were out of our minds," company president Don Ross says. "They felt that giving up our most valuable commodity—our people—was wrong. But every time we put an employee in a claims center, our business skyrocketed. We helped manage a piece of business for our insurance clients that can be costly if not done well. They rewarded us by sending more rentals our way."

Automobile accidents are divided into two categories: drivable and non-drivable. A drivable accident is one where a car is damaged but can still be driven until the repairs are made. A non-drivable accident occurs when the vehicle is damaged so badly, it must be towed to the nearest body shop directly from an accident scene. According to industry figures, 30 percent of all accidents are drivable; 70 percent are not.

In drivable accidents, policyholders usually contact their insurance company (or the responsible party's carrier) to file a claim. At this point, the adjuster takes the appropriate notes, issues a claim number, and goes into the ARMS system to reserve an Enterprise car. They'll note in the reservation what the policy covers in terms of the per-day rate and length of rental, so Enterprise knows what has been approved. The reservation then automatically prints out at the appropriate branch.

In non-drivable accidents, customers frequently drive in the tow truck (assuming no one has been hurt) to the body shop before calling Enterprise directly or at the suggestion of body shop personnel. Building relationships with these body shops is another important job at Enterprise, since such referrals provide a steady stream of business. In these instances, policyholders frequently show up at the Enterprise office before contacting their insurance company. As part of the overall service, Enterprise employees offer to call the insurance provider on the customer's behalf, seeking approval for the rental. It's akin to a reverse reservation. If for any reason the insurance company doesn't agree to pay for the rental, it becomes the customer's responsibility.

In a fairly short time, a significant percentage of all insurance companies signed on with Enterprise to use ARMS. A new iteration was launched on the Internet in 1999, making it much easier for insurance partners to connect to. Enterprise sent out its national insurance marketing managers to set up the connections and show insurers how to use the system. With connections easier to make, demand for the technology grew as it was adapted to even more uses. Body and repair shops could log in electronically to note repair progress through what became known as ARMS Automotive, preventing the need for Enterprise employees to constantly call by phone for updates. At the group level, Enterprise created a team of Enterprise Technology Experts, or ETEs. One person in each group became an expert on how to use ARMS and was then charged with training other users in their local area. Today there are about 200 ETEs companywide, and another 800 Enterprise employees who work inside insurance companies helping them to manage this process.

The open-ticket reporting feature of ARMS gives insurance companies a real-time view of every open rental and joins together the other sophisticated reporting data ARMS offered: directional trends, closed and open tickets, and a look at how inventories stack up. For the first time, insurers could dig down to the macro level, analyzing information from all sides and getting detailed reports on, for example, which adjusters kept rentals open the longest and which ones closed them out the fastest.

As a testament to how effective this has been for both sides, a few years back one insurance company gave its Employee of the Month Award to an on-site Enterprise manager who saved the company significant money through the implementation of ARMS.

Find Creative Ways to
Save Your Partners Money

With the rollout of ARMS under way, Enterprise took another step to deepen its insurance partner relationships through the creation of preferred provider option agreements, or PPOs. These agreements serve as written understandings of what new additional value-added services Enterprise would bring to the table in exchange for suggesting Enterprise to customers with no other preference.

"Really all these agreements do is go through and list what services we'll perform for the insurance companies," Ross explains. "It details the things we believe we bring to the market that differentiate us because of who we are and where we're located. In a technical sense, it is an agreement that they'll do business with us, and in some cases they may be agreeing to give us a possibly larger share of rentals in exchange for our complete program of ARMS technology, efficient reporting, superior service, well-developed branch network, competitive pricing, and, of course, our people. But we still constantly have to earn their business."

Before ARMS, as the two sides began to talk and negotiate an agreement, insurance companies often tried to get Enterprise to lower its per-day rental rates. But Enterprise had a better solution. Rather than taking $1 a day off the cost of the daily rental, the company pledged that ARMS would help its insurance partners cut back even further on the average number of days each replacement car was rented, saving considerably more money in the long run.

"We said, 'If you lower the rate by $1 a day on a fourteen-day rental, you'll only save $14,'" Ross recalls. "Instead, we'll show you how to cut back on the length of the rental, bringing it down from fourteen days, to thirteen days, and eventually twelve days. That will allow for even more significant savings."

This was possible because of the in-depth management and reporting process available through ARMS. As promised, by 2005 Enterprise's average rental length for the replacement fleet had dropped from fourteen days to nearly twelve days. In other words, the system was working as intended, while laying to rest fears that allowing Enterprise to manage the entire process was like putting the fox in charge of the henhouse. Although Enterprise would have benefited from keeping cars rented longer, doing so would ruin its credibility with the insurance industry. By demonstrating that it really was able to create efficiencies and save its partners money, the company's overall insurance business has increased dramatically over the past decade.

"The reason we've grown so much and earned more business is because we've built the most cost-effective and best infrastructure. Plus, we offer excellent customer service," says Ross. "Part of this comes from the fact that we are able to deliver a scope of services that our insurance partners were never exposed to before. They are amazed at the lengths our branches will go to please them."

"Enterprise was the first rental car company to really understand that getting more transactions automated would save everybody money," adds Brian Passell, claims president for Progressive. "They had to drag some people in kicking and screaming. But they were visionary in saying that when you don't make a lot of money per transaction, you better not waste anything. We can now set up reservations through ARMS without talking to anybody. It's really a seamless process."

Continually Strive for Greater Efficiencies

The evolution of the ARMS system continues. As recently as three years ago, hard copies of all invoices for rentals were still sent to insurance companies through the mail, with individual checks being mailed back to Enterprise offices for processing. It was an expensive proposition. The cost of processing a single check for an insurance company is estimated to range from $20 to $40. With some insurance partners renting more than 1 million cars annually for policyholders, this represented a significant hit to the bottom line. In response, Enterprise configured ARMS to enable insurance providers to be invoiced and make payments electronically, saving them lots of money. As a result, Enterprise avoids having to mail out some 6 million invoices a year and gets paid faster. Simply put, everyone wins. What's more, there's rarely a dispute about whether a rental has been authorized by the insurance company, since there are tracking notes in ARMS about each rental.

Enterprise spends about $10 million annually on system upgrades to ARMS. Some 300 insurance companies now use

ARMS. An affiliated application, ARMS for Dealerships, connects several thousand car dealers around the country to Enterprise, while ARMS Automotive is used by some 7,000 body shops. This enables Enterprise to send queries on the status of customer repairs and receive updates electronically, reducing the long-running games of telephone tag that formerly characterized the process. If a repair takes longer than anticipated, the insurance company is notified of this through ARMS. Once the repair is completed and the rental car returned, ARMS automatically generates an invoice, which is sent to the insurer.

Seven managers head the national sales organization overseeing the insurance business at Enterprise headquarters. They divide up the 200 biggest insurers in the United States, focusing largely on the top 100. Four technology managers report to the national sales department. The goal is to assure that Enterprise maintains a strategic business solution for every insurance company. This department develops the agreements for each insurer, setting rates and other variables. An agreement can take days or years to negotiate. Once it is concluded, this department maintains the relationship and makes sure Enterprise lives up to its commitments.

But even with corporate-wide agreements in place with insurance companies at the regional and national levels, the system works well only if local execution is solid.

"If our local managers deliver great service to an insurance company's policyholder during a time of need, everyone wins," chief operating officer Pam Nicholson says. "So whether we are negotiating a corporate-wide plan or ensuring that a policyholder is treated with respect and care at the branch level, it's all about relationship building."

"We have more than 20,000 rental managers in our branch network working every day to ensure that all customers are treated right—whether they come to us as an insurance company referral or as a consumer across town," Ross adds. "It's all about local management."

Andy Taylor insists that the key contributor to the company's success with the insurance industry is that Enterprise is not just a rental car company. "We provide solutions and reduce the costs associated with the rental process," he says. "We offer a sophisticated value proposition to our customers in what is otherwise a commodity-driven business."

"The simple truth is that all of us listened to our core customers and wanted to give them an avenue for doing business in a much simpler and more efficient way," Nicholson notes.

As an extension of the rental relationship with insurers, Enterprise's retail car sales division has embarked on a new initiative to help insurance customers whose vehicles are a total loss as a result of an accident. Under the program, adjusters suggest Enterprise Car Sales to their total-loss customers. They are given the name and number of a local coordinator, who puts them in touch with an Enterprise account executive. "This is a new way of doing business that we call Total Loss Solutions," Andy Taylor says. "A customer whose vehicle is destroyed in an accident is in a tough spot, and the adjuster needs help finding a remedy. We aim to provide a solution that gives customers a great resale car at a fair price."

"We are developing this type of pilot program with a number of insurance partners," Ross adds. "The most important thing is making sure these relationships are beneficial to all parties: the insurance companies, Enterprise, and the mutual customers we serve."

Be Good Stewards on Behalf of Your Partners

Beyond the business and functional side, there's another crucial component to Enterprise's partnership with insurance companies. Enterprise is not only the company providing policyholders with a replacement car, often it is the public face these customers see during a very difficult time, usually following an automobile accident.

Claims are frequently filed by phone, and sometimes there is no in-person contact with the insurance company at all. As a result, Enterprise employees often represent the insurance company, too. How they treat customers, therefore, reflects on many different parties. That's why Enterprise employees must consistently put their best foot forward, not only for Enterprise, but for the referring party, as well.

"The most common compliment I get is that all of Enterprise's people are so nice," adds Seth Ingall, vice president of claims for Geico. "It's the people that make any organization a wonderful, service-oriented company. In the case of Enterprise, they just get it from the top down. They deliver the car with a smile on their faces, they present well, and there aren't issues that might ordinarily surface with another provider."

"In this capacity, we really are an extension of the insurer," Andy Taylor says. "We teach our people to say things like 'Gee, I'm really sorry you had an accident this morning. We want to tell you that our experience is that your insurance company does a great job of settling their claims, and I'm sure that is not going to be an issue for you. Our main concern is getting you into an appropriate car that will satisfy your needs, and we'll do it fast so you can get back to work or wherever you need to go.' We then follow through on the whole process, making sure both Enterprise and the insurance company do a good job of taking care of the customers."

With Progressive, Enterprise is trying a new kind of partnership. Progressive's Concierge service allows customers to drop off their cars at a Progressive location. The Progressive employee takes the customer's keys, gives them an Enterprise car that has already been delivered to the office, drives the damaged vehicle to a preselected body shop (saving customers the hassle of going around for estimates), and then inspects all repairs before giving the car back. In this case, Progressive policyholders never deal with anyone but a Progressive employee.

"Enterprise had some reservations about the Concierge service at first because they felt they needed to be involved with the customer," Passell admits. "It was almost a deal breaker in the early stages, because they felt we were messing up the customer service experience for them." Passell arranged a meeting between Progressive CEO Glenn Renwick and Andy Taylor to discuss how the two sides could effectively work together. "To their credit, they decided this was a different way of looking at things and might be the wave of insurance in the future," Passell says. "It has worked very well so far."

Negotiate as Friends

Beyond the insurance companies and body shops, Enterprise also has numerous business relationships with the auto manufacturers that supply its vehicles. Enterprise has its own PPO agreements with several carmakers and, as noted earlier, is one of the largest customers of both General Motors and Ford. It also buys a great many cars from DaimlerChrysler, and a full one-third of its vehicles are purchased from a variety of other manufacturers.

"It's important to have relationships with many carmakers, since we purchase 600,000-plus vehicles each year in the United States alone," Nicholson says. "We need a variety of models to make sure we're getting the highest residual value when it comes time to remarket these vehicles." It's estimated that Enterprise buys between 3 percent and 5 percent of all vehicles produced in America each year, making it the largest private purchaser of new cars in the world.

"There's definitely some negotiation involved to make sure we get the best transaction possible, but we make certain we're always amicable partners at the end," Nicholson says. "We find ways to come to an agreement based on their needs, what works for us, and taking into account any current and expected future incentives.

"There have even been times when automakers came to us and said, 'Business is a bit slow and we're trying to build as many cars as we can to keep the plants running. We have a few weeks' worth of production available on a particular model and wonder whether you're interested in buying that inventory,'" Nicholson shares. Such arrangements allow Enterprise to save money while preventing factories from having to close temporarily.

To take the partnership with automakers a step further, Enterprise arranges to have the cars delivered and sold from local dealerships near each branch. This supports the community, keeps tax dollars local, and helps to strengthen relationships between the dealerships and nearby Enterprise branches.

In turn, Enterprise is often the preferred provider of loaner cars for these dealerships. In many cases, the agreement calls for Enterprise to supply customers of the dealership with loaners made by that same manufacturer. For instance, Enterprise has an arrangement with General Motors to put customers of GM dealerships into loaner cars made by GM. It has similar relationships with various other manufacturers as well. At many dealerships, Enterprise has a rental office right on site. Otherwise, one is close by, and employees are in regular contact to see that enough cars are available to take care of demand and that customer pick-ups are prompt.

When it comes time to remarket those cars, Enterprise often sells them back to the dealers they were purchased from, to put on their used car lots. "They have come to count on us to have those cars available," Nicholson says. "We have sort of a virtual inventory for them. Some dealers will call and say, 'I need ten of this model in this particular color with a certain amount of mileage.' We'll go through our fleet and find these vehicles. The dealers know that if one of the cars shows up on the lot with a scratch or dent or something we didn't describe, we'll take it back and get them something else."

Form Synergistic Alliances

Another example of effective partnering can be seen in the long-standing relationship between Enterprise's retail car sales division (known as referral sales) and various credit unions. Credit union referrals account for about 30 percent of all such sales. At one point, Enterprise promoted its retail used car sales the traditional way: through local advertising. Although its no-haggle policy set the company apart, the approach wasn't much different from that of dealerships. This started to change in 1985, when Don Ross led a charge to approach the Missouri Credit Union League in St. Louis with the idea of staging a one-day car sales event for its members.

"That first special sale proved to be extremely successful," Ross recalls. "We immediately realized how valuable credit union partnerships were and soon held more one-day events in other groups around the country."

The arrangement benefits both sides. The credit unions give

Enterprise access to members, while the credit union makes a margin on the car loans taken out to finance these purchases. This is additionally attractive to the credit unions, since 40 percent of all loans granted by these institutions are for automobiles. When members go out and buy a car on their own, they often finance through the dealership instead. "Our sales kept the financing business with the credit unions," Ross says.

More recently, the company began working with its 800-plus credit union partners to leverage the growing online car shopping phenomenon by developing content tailored to those members looking to buy new vehicles on the Web. Members are linked from the credit union's homepage to a co-branded Enterprise Car Sales site, where they can sort available vehicles by year, make, model, price, mileage, color, and location. The technology also gives members a detailed review of the vehicles, including photos, features, interior and exterior colors, and VIN numbers.

Once a member locates a vehicle, he or she can use the Web site to investigate and pursue financing from the credit union (the only lending option available through the site), and even fill out an application. In another example of setting up a win-win partnership, Enterprise guarantees that the credit unions receive 100 percent of all car loans made through the site 100 percent of the time.

Six Keys to Forming Effective Partnerships

What has Enterprise done to create such close and mutually beneficial partnerships over the years? The same things that every business can do to achieve similar results.

1. Begin by identifying the concerns of your customers and potential partners. In the case of ARMS, Enterprise started by asking what was important to the insurance companies it worked with. It would have been easy not to create a system that made the rental process more efficient, since that cut into Enterprise's business. But such thinking would have been short-sighted. "We went into it saying we want to win a little bit and we want you to win a lot," Ross says. "They said we need to reduce our total cost per transaction and we're having a hard time managing the repair shops. We listened to their problems and came up with a solution. We didn't think about the cost of doing this. We just did it." In exchange, Enterprise earned unbelievable loyalty and received significant new business from these satisfied insurers.

2. Once you've identified what your partners want, determine the mutual benefits from the relationship. Remember, this is designed to be a good arrangement for both sides. Enterprise built ARMS to help its insurance partners save money through shorter rentals, but it had faith that the strategy would prove successful in the form of additional business down the line. "You can't just do everything you or your partner wants, because then the deal is purely one-sided," Nicholson observes. "You've got to identify what you both need and say, 'I'll do this for you, but here's what I need in return.' It's the classic win-win situation. If you're both winning, then you have a true partnership."

3. Believe in what you say you are going to do and go into the relationship with a 100 percent commitment. That was a challenge when Enterprise first introduced ARMS. Many branches were skeptical about whether it would work, especially since they weren't asking the insurance companies for any commitments of business in return. But Enterprise executives believed the plan was the right thing to do and would lead to long-term loyalty and additional business. They turned out to be right.

4. Don't go for the last "oink out of the pig." It's common for businesses to walk into partnerships and negotiations focused solely on how they can come away with the very best deal possible. When hammering out pricing terms, for instance, it's tempting to go back and forth trying to squeeze out every last penny of advantage. Enterprise takes a longer view, emphasizing where it would like the relationship to be over the next fifteen years, instead of the next fifteen months. "I like to tell our people that it's not about getting the last oink out of the pig," Andy Taylor says. "That doesn't mean we don't negotiate hard, or that we never have issues with our partners. But we try to always work together, even in areas where we disagree, to work toward a common goal."

5. Keep the lines of communication fluid and open. "Generally, all good partnerships will succeed or fail because of communication," says Geico's Ingall, whose company recently renewed its PPO agreement with Enterprise for several more years. "One reason the partnership with Enterprise works is because there is constant and frequent communication between our two companies, and it's generally aimed at the customer experience."

It is essential to have a solid understanding of what your business partners need, combined with regular communication to determine how you can best work with them to achieve their goals.

"We always have our eye on where the hockey puck is going to be and not just chasing it," Andy Taylor says. "We ask questions like: How can we add more value for you? How can we help your business? What more can we provide to make your business easier?"

6. Never rest on your laurels. Once you have a deal with your business partners, you must keep re-earning their trust all the time. "At the end of the day, even with the PPO agreements in place, nothing would stop any one of our customers from kicking us out the door if we weren't providing the right kind of service and taking care of their needs," Ross admits.

"Other rental companies frequently call looking to steal away some of our rental car business," says Geico's Ingall. "While I haven't found anyone else that can replicate what they do, Enterprise always has to keep working, as do we, to keep our customers happy in order to maintain our business."

Progressive's Passell maintains that what impresses him most about Enterprise is how humble the company is. "In spite of the fact that Enterprise owns such a significant percentage of the insurance replacement business, it still strives to continually exceed customer expectations," he says. "Even though it's the gigantic elephant of rental car companies, Enterprise wants to get better and is always willing to learn new things."

THE ENTERPRISE WAY

1. Successful partnerships are based on building long-term relationships.
2. Establish customized win-win arrangements with your major customers and partners. Then figure out how to capitalize on the synergies between your companies to the benefit of your mutual customers.
3. Consistently look for ways of adding value to the products and services you bring to the partnership, both now and in the future.

4. One way to increase business is by developing methods for *reducing* the amount of money your partners spend with you per transaction. While that might seem counterintuitive and can lead to a short-term hit, demonstrating your commitment to cutting their costs will earn their loyalty and likely give you a bigger chunk of their overall business in the future.

5. Automation can be an effective way to increase efficiencies for both you and your partners, especially if you provide the appropriate training to ensure that everyone knows how to properly use such systems.

6. When partners come to you looking for solutions, always listen to their needs and figure out how you can meet them. At the same time, don't be afraid to share your challenges, since a true effective partnership benefits both sides.

7. While the goal of every negotiation is to get the best transaction possible, be certain to come out of these discussions as partners for the long term, instead of trying to squeeze out the last possible concession.

8. Keep the lines of communication open between you and your partners, sharing concerns and double-checking to see whether you are meeting their needs. If not, figure out why and come up with ways to fix what's broken.

9. Once a partnership is in place, remember that you must constantly work to keep it going. There are many alternatives for customers to choose from. If you don't keep your partners happy, they'll leave.

$$\overline{7}$$

Use Technology to Enhance the Customer Experience

WHILE ENTERPRISE HAS clearly built its business on offering the personal touch to employees, customers, and business partners alike, it has long been a pioneer in the use of technology to enhance its operations and improve the overall customer experience. The company discovered long ago that no matter how good your product or service, without the smart use of technology, you'll lose out on the opportunity to make it easy and cost-effective for customers to do business with you. Enterprise's overall technology architecture is built to prevent downtime and improve efficiencies while making certain the rental process for every individual is as convenient and seamless as possible.

"That's important, because customers don't want to hear that you can't take care of them because of computer problems, and it's crucial to use technology as a way of making an individual's dealings with you even more pleasurable," says company president Don Ross.

Have Programmers Spend Time
Learning the Business

Enterprise's overriding philosophy is that, above all, technology should be used as a way to drive customer service. Among other things, this means making sure that programmers are always in close alignment with those running all aspects of the business operation. To that end, when the company hired its first chief technology officer in 1973, instead of having him immediately get started on writing code, Jack Taylor sent him out to work in the field for nine months. This way he could observe and partic-ipate in lease operations, rent cars at branch offices, meet with Enterprise employees, and learn the nitty-gritty side of the com-pany's business. It was Jack's belief that the only way the program-mer could develop a computerized system useful to every aspect of the operation was by getting a firsthand understanding of how the company worked. If he didn't know what the rental process was like for a customer, for instance, how could he possibly write a program for making it more customer-friendly and efficient?

Admittedly, Enterprise's early automation efforts, like those of most other companies, were more inwardly focused. In other words, they looked primarily at how technology could help to improve the speed of various processes, such as accounting, man-aging the payroll, and tracking inventories. This also spoke to the inherent limitations of early computer systems, which were often more like glorified calculators than the superpowerful machines we have come to know today.

However, what distinguished Enterprise from others and paved the way for impressive future innovations was the fact that Jack and Andy Taylor, along with many others from senior manage-ment, fully supported the various IT initiatives from the start and were involved in all phases of development. To this day, the company's top officers sit on a committee that helps to guide and prioritize Enterprise's technological needs.

"More than anything else, we believe that technology for its own sake is irrelevant," insists Andy Taylor. "It's only relevant if it is solving a business problem or customer service issue. It is about empowering our employees to serve our customers. And when it comes to deciding whether to go forward with an initiative, if it's something that we are convinced will lead to taking better care of our customers, it moves to the top of our priority list, usually regardless of cost."

Indeed, Enterprise looks at technology as a strategic asset—something that can help to strengthen the customer relationship—and not just as another cost of doing business.

"We do forecast expenses every year, but we do not set a specific technology budget per se," Andy Taylor says. "If someone comes up with an idea that will help us improve customer service or bring a strategic advantage, we'll do a quick calculation and usually tell them to go ahead and do it. We won't turn down a good idea just because it's not in the budget."

Use Technology to Deliver Better Customer Service

For many years, the rental transaction at Enterprise was purely a manual process. Tickets were written by hand, cars were tracked on chalkboards, and detailed customer information was jotted on plain index cards. Each time Enterprise took a serious look at creating the kind of all-encompassing computerized rental system it has now, the vast complexity of the task seemed to hold back progress. But as the glut of paperwork on the rental side kept growing, threatening to divert attention away from customer service, it was clear that too much time was being spent on filing reports and checking numbers. Without question, something needed to be done.

In the mid-1980s, at the urging of one insightful city manager, Andy Taylor agreed that it was essential to start automating many of these functions for the sake of the company's customers.

"Employees were writing contracts on clipboards," he recalls. "They would stand in front of customers, looking down at the paper the whole time and not even making eye contact with them. This was no longer acceptable. What's more, when we decided to automate these functions, we didn't even look at the return on investment. We just knew that building the necessary systems would strengthen our interactions with customers, and that was reason enough to go forward with it."

This whole mandate proved to be a watershed event for the company, ushering in a change of focus from viewing technology as a way of improving internal processes to an effective tool for taking better care of customers.

Ultimately, a prototype rental application project got the green light, with St. Louis and Kansas City chosen for a limited test run of a new system called ECARS: Enterprise Computer Assisted Rental System.

The first edition of ECARS was basically used to simply open and close a rental ticket. But it proved successful from the start. During the initial trial period, Enterprise measured the time spent on transactions using the system and other performance parameters, and saw the improvement in customer service that ECARS could help its employees achieve. The ultimate decision on whether to deploy the system nationwide wasn't based on metrics, but rather on the impressions of the company's top managers. Was it improving service? Did employees prefer using the automated terminals over the manual method?

The response was unanimous: Yes, it was determined, ECARS should be implemented throughout the company's entire rental operation. Over time, those employees in the field working on the front lines started asking for additional enhancements to help improve the customer experience further. Among other things, analysis and reporting tools were built in. In relatively short order, the application evolved into the kind of integrated system Enterprise wanted when it decided to automate in the first place.

But how would the company get all of its branches around the country connected? Initially, each office was plugged into a host-based system in St. Louis by telephone lines. But this created some real challenges. To open a new office, Enterprise was dependent on the phone company to set up service, which could take several weeks or even months. And given that there was only one terrestrial provider in each city, Enterprise had only a single option to choose from.

"That was just totally unacceptable to us," notes Ross. "We had people in the field saying, 'There's a great opportunity to serve our customers by opening a new branch or by moving to a new location.' We were opening two locations each business day, and we needed to get these offices up and running as fast as possible. We could no longer keep waiting for the phone companies to fit us into their schedules. In addition, every construction crew with a backhoe was a threat to our branch network's ability to connect to our offices."

This frustration led Enterprise to embrace a satellite network. Branches were equipped with a small (36 inches wide by 24 inches high) parabolic antenna that sent and received data through a satellite hanging in orbit 22,000 miles above the earth. Enterprise's data center in St. Louis was equipped with a much larger antenna (about 20 feet in diameter) to accommodate sending and receiving from the various offices and devices. The satellite system allowed the company to open a branch in as little as twenty-four hours, and reliability was excellent.

Going to the satellite system was a unique proposition, especially for a company of Enterprise's size.

"Satellite leases required a huge up-front financial commitment, though we were not driven by cost," Andy Taylor emphasizes. "What drove us to make this investment is we were not able to respond to our customers and the need to open new branches fast enough. Satellites were more scalable and eventually a more cost-effective way to connect with our operations."

Enhance Communications

With the rollout of ECARS in full swing, Enterprise's IT department figured out another way for all locations to be connected and share important data with one another. It created an early form of e-mail that enabled employees to easily send text messages to specific individuals throughout the company.

Some executives were initially reluctant to add this feature to ECARS. They wondered: Why not just have employees pick up the phone instead of sending a text message? Nevertheless, the objective did fit in with the company's value of keeping everyone working together and sharing information. Once the messaging application was approved and implemented, it became the most heavily used program on the system and further underscored the value computerization brought to the company. In a time of rapid expansion, communication was critical in order for everyone to remain on the same page.

"For the first time, our messaging system gave all employees a chance to instantly talk to their colleagues around the world and share their best practices for customer service," Andy Taylor observes. "We could also send out announcements and share important information. At the same time, our programmers were in regular contact with frontline employees to get insights into ways for enhancing our solutions. After all, the most innovative ideas on how systems should perform come from those employees who are actually out there directly serving our customers."

More important, this messaging system provided the basis for building a more comprehensive national reservations system and further served as the cornerstone for developing ARMS, the insurance partnership tool highlighted in Chapter 6.

"By ensuring that our data and systems were all in sync, we were able to more easily take on national insurance accounts, online reservations, corporate accounts, and national reservations," says Ross. "We made our foray into electronic commerce long before there was any talk about the Internet, and we developed our system specifically in order to better respond to our customers."

The initial incarnation of ECARS was in full deployment by 1989. As managers used it, they kept coming up with new ideas on how the system could be enhanced to more effectively serve both employees and customers. Because of the close coordination between the field and the IT department, these ideas could be tested and evaluated, and new capabilities were continually being added.

Several enhancements were made based on ideas generated in the field. Among other things, if someone wanted to rent a specific type of car that a branch didn't have, an employee could quickly determine which other nearby location had one available so it could satisfy that customer's need. The system was also built to store other customer preferences, handle split billing (cases where an insurance company is paying for only part of a rental), and even calculate any deductions applied from the customer service account.

Keep Up with the Times

ECARS began to show its age as the 1990s progressed. It was designed with a shelf life of about ten years and had more than reached that milestone. The company wasn't convinced that the implemented features alone were doing enough to really improve the overall rental experience. At the same time, it was discovered that those workers most adept at inputting data into computers seemed to get the biggest promotions, even though all that typing didn't necessarily improve customer service in a quantifiable way. It had become clear that ECARS was designed as a customer *transaction* system, and now a customer *relationship* program was needed.

"This wasn't how it was supposed to work," Andy Taylor reflects. "It turned out that some people were putting a lot of data into the system, but they weren't doing an effective job of taking care of our customers."

That's one of the reasons why Enterprise set out to implement ECARS 2.0, complete with new features allowing employees to use technology to take better care of customers. It also provides an improved fleet management tool, so branches can better utilize the vehicles assigned to them.

ECARS 2.0 gives branch employees critical information needed to take care of the more than 35 million customers that Enterprise serves each year. The new reservation system is intuitive, with navigation tabs that make it easy to move through the process quickly in any order an employee wants, in turn bypassing unneeded screens. But this streamlined functionality created a dilemma. Sending data via satellite causes a three-to-four-second delay in response. While that wasn't bad when employees merely used the system to fill out rental forms, as the capabilities increased, this delay really added to the time it took to gather and input information. Therefore, Enterprise once again pushed aside cost in deciding to move away from satellites in favor of setting up a private virtual network connected through multiple T1 lines.

"The truth is, terrestrial network providers have dramatically changed from where they were just a few years ago," Ross observes. "There is now much more competition, and we are able to get the lines set up faster, although we still worry about those construction crews and their backhoes."

In addition, in this era of deregulation, costs have significantly dropped, and Enterprise has numerous providers to choose from, lessening the risk of being reliant on a single company.

"We generally use at least two providers in a given area, so if one has a failure, we can reroute traffic by switching over to another carrier," Nicholson says. "That wasn't possible in the past. If your one provider had a problem, you were in the dark until things were back up and running."

Involve Everyone from Top to Bottom

One major difference among the systems used by Enterprise and its major competitors is that Enterprise writes and develops all of the technology applications used to take care of customer needs in-house. Most other companies rely heavily on outside consultants and independent contractors, many of whom don't know the car rental business very well.

"Our belief is that you should focus your energy internally on building custom-designed technology solutions that address strategic, customer-focused needs," says Ross. "If you're just looking to perform common business activities, such as accounting and general ledger functions, you might as well buy an off-the-shelf program, since it's hard to add much additional value from what's already available."

With an IT staff of more than 1,400, Enterprise no longer sends programmers out to work in the field, given the disruption having all those people in the branches would cause. However, it still makes sure programmers have a clear understanding of the business and customer needs. One way this is accomplished is by dividing programmers into application teams by business area. For instance, there are separate teams devoted to serving the needs of rental, national reservations, fleet services, ARMS, and so forth. Programmers on these teams work directly with liaisons from the various departments to get a greater education into how these individual operations work and what their specific business needs are. At the same time, the programmers help these department heads to better understand the capabilities of the IT function.

"We have representatives on each of these teams who are responsible for gathering the business requirements by engaging those in the field," Ross explains. "They then present these requirements to the IT folks, who manage the process of developing the application. Once an application is finalized, it is tested. After we've determined it works and is reliable, the representatives on the business side are responsible for creating and delivering any needed training in the field."

Enterprise believes that it's crucial for IT professionals to continuously work together with those executives closest to the business and its customers.

"It's very easy for companies to allow their technology people to work in a vacuum," Andy Taylor observes. "When that happens, they wind up solving technology problems instead of business problems. At the same time, nontechnical businesspeople may not understand what technology can and cannot do. That's why the two sides must work together and have a common purpose and understanding. They need to know their real purpose is to serve the customer with technology. After all, we're not in the technology business. We're here to serve our customers."

"It's also important not to forget who your customers are," Ross adds. "Some IT people feel the customer is the department head they report to, or even the business liaison they work with. The person at corporate *isn't* your customer. The real customer is the person at the counter trying to rent a car, and the Enterprise employee helping in that process."

Enterprise's first System 38 computer back in the late 1970s cost about $20,000. Today, the company's annual hardware budget alone is $30 million. The information technology department spends well in excess of $250 million per year. Enterprise's pioneering information technology efforts have been recognized by many, including *CIO* magazine.

Because of the specialized needs of this department, a majority of Enterprise's IT employees come from outside the company, although there are a number of exceptions. While programmers receive a salary competitive with the market, many IT managers are paid off of the bottom line, giving them an added incentive to create automated solutions that continuously enhance the overall customer experience, thus allowing them to share in the same risk as business managers. More important, all programmers are allowed to work with the latest technologies and are given regular training, and nearly everyone in the department is promoted from within. In fact, Enterprise's current chief technology officer started as a programmer. As a result, the company's IT department has a retention rate of more than 90 percent and has had only three CIOs in its history, which is quite impressive for a profession where turnover is famously high.

THE ENTERPRISE WAY

1. Above all, technology should be used as a way to drive customer service.
2. In order for a technology initiative to really work, it must have clearly defined goals and objectives and be embraced from the top of the company down.
3. Ensure that programmers work closely with executives of each department within the business, so they'll have a thorough understanding of how the technology will be used and can therefore produce applications better suited to taking good care of your customers.
4. Technology for its own sake is irrelevant. It only matters if it is solving a business problem, resolving a customer service issue, or creating a competitive advantage.
5. Allow technology to automate routine manual functions that don't require human interaction, giving you and your employees more time to deliver excellent personalized service.
6. Avoid setting rigid budgets. Allow for flexibility as new solutions are invented that can bring you a strategic advantage.
7. Custom-designed IT solutions should address strategic, customer-focused needs. If you're simply looking to per-

form common business activities, such as accounting functions, you are better off buying an off-the-shelf program.

8. ROI should not be the only factor in deciding whether to build or support customized automated systems, especially if the programs will serve to enhance a customer's overall experience with you.

9. Utilize automated systems to foster and enhance communications among employees spread out over large areas or even countries.

10. Let the needs of your business and customers drive decisions about how technology should be applied.

11. As with your other employees, it makes sense to pay your IT management team off of the bottom line.

Grow Smart

YOU MIGHT SAY that Andy Taylor was the right man at the right place at the right time. Although his father founded Enterprise, it was on Andy's watch that the company experienced such explosive growth. Like everyone else at the company, Andy began by working his way up. Though he is the founder's son, he has been a brilliant leader in his own right.

"It was important for me to pave my own path," Andy says. "My father built the foundation of the business, and I helped take it to the next level."

At the time Andy was appointed president in 1980, Enterprise had about 14,000 cars on lease and some 5,000 rental vehicles, with revenues of less than $80 million and operations in about a dozen cities across four states. Today, thanks largely to initiatives Andy put into action, Enterprise has 160,000-plus leased cars and more than 700,000 rental vehicles, with revenues about to surpass $9 billion and operations in five different countries.

Andy recognized the potential for turning Enterprise into an industry-leading company relatively early on. "I saw the power in our business model of having this highly incentivized confederation of branches with a common set of values and getting things done as small teams," he explains. "I was sold right away on the fact that this could become a national—and perhaps even global—company. I think my dad was more conservative about this view than me."

Andy likes to joke that he and Jack are lucky their birth order worked out the way it did. "Jack [Andy always refers to his dad as Jack to avoid setting himself apart from other employees] admittedly didn't have the kind of management skills I do to run a multibillion-dollar company," Andy says. "At the same time, I'm not sure I could have taken a 50 percent pay cut like he did to start Enterprise from scratch. He had flown off an aircraft carrier and watched some of his friends get shot down, so the move of starting a business wasn't a huge risk to him. He figured he could get a job someplace else if it didn't work out. I probably wouldn't have done that. Jack told me, 'Andy, I loved starting the business. That did not seem like a huge risk for me. But I'm not the manager you are. If you hadn't come along, there's no way the company would have grown the way it has.' It turned out to be a perfect combination. Jack never wanted to be a detail manager. He's an entrepreneurial guy, and long-term growth strategies were not necessarily the first things on his list."

Give Yourself an Out

Although Enterprise experienced impressive growth during the two decades Jack was at the helm, he always took a more cautious approach to building the business. Jack carefully considered the cost of each new move and calculated the potential losses if things didn't work out. "Before doing anything, I'd ask, 'What is the downside risk? How badly can we be hurt? If it goes bad, can we digest the loss without it affecting our future?'" Jack says. "If we determined we could survive it and it was something I or others thought was a worthwhile venture, we'd go for it."

Not surprisingly, Jack was reluctant to sign long-term leases in case things didn't work exactly as planned. This apprehension led to the birth of the "JCT Clause," something Enterprise still occasionally uses. The JCT (for Jack C. Taylor) Clause dates back to the early 1970s. At the time, the company's strategy called for expanding primarily into secondary markets, since Jack felt the competition was too stiff in some of the larger top-tier cities. "The competition could eat us alive," he was known to admonish managers when the subject of opening a branch in a large metro area came up. Among other things, Jack wasn't sure whether Enterprise's friendly Midwestern approach would go over well in crowded and fast-paced big cities. Nevertheless, the manager of the Florida operation, Lanny Dacus, had his eye on expanding into Fort Lauderdale in the early 1970s. Dacus found what appeared to be the ideal spot for an Enterprise branch: an empty Krystal restaurant. The owner of the former hamburger joint wanted $1,000 a month in rent and a five-year lease commitment. While Jack agreed it was a good location, he was reluctant to commit to the five-year term, given Fort Lauderdale's proximity to the much larger and more competitive Miami market.

Jack sat down with the property owner and explained his apprehension, and the two agreed on an addendum to the lease that would henceforth be known as the JCT Clause. It stipulated that Enterprise could get out of its lease with ninety days' notice and payment of an additional ninety days, or three months, of rent. This became a boilerplate in almost every branch lease the company negotiated, and it is one of the ways the company limited risk early on as it grew into new areas and locations.

Beware of Quick Profits

In the early days, some managers were frustrated by Jack's overly cautious stance on growth, although they later came to see the value of his go-slow approach—often after learning some hard lessons. One of the most notable also took place in the Sunshine State in the mid-1970s. The millions of visitors who came to Orlando to visit Walt Disney World generally didn't benefit Enterprise, since it wasn't targeting tourists. But one day the manager of a nearby Alamo Rent-A-Car phoned the city's newest Enterprise branch, which was relatively close to the airport, to see if it could help out with some of Alamo's overflow. The branch was more than happy to oblige. It was mid-February, the heart of the tourist season, and Alamo was overbooked by 600 cars.

Since this particular Enterprise branch was just getting started, it had only thirteen vehicles available. Because Alamo needed more, the branch manager called all over Florida trying to round up as many cars as possible from other Enterprise offices. He saw this as his opportunity to make a big splash. For weeks, a huge Alamo bus would show up at the Enterprise branch several times a day, dropping off somewhat confused travelers who weren't sure why they were being handed over to some then-unknown car rental company. The Enterprise staffers greeted everyone personally, explaining that the rate promised by Alamo would remain the same and giving them a taste of Enterprise's customer-focused service. As Alamo kept overbooking and Enterprise continued to keep its customers happy, the branch started breaking sales records, becoming operationally profitable in its first month. Profits zoomed even higher in March and climbed further as Easter weekend approached. The Enterprise branch decided to close on Easter Sunday in order to give managers a day off to savor their good fortune.

The following Monday morning, this celebratory mood ended as the exodus of tourists northward out of Florida got into full swing. Every car the branch had out on rent was returned that day. The Enterprise lot overflowed with parked cars. It got so bad, the bevy of vehicles blocked access to a nearby residential neighborhood. This once-thriving Enterprise branch now had scores of idle cars, and the Alamo bus was no longer showing up with extra business. Managers started calling other Enterprise branches where the cars came from, pleading with them to take the vehicles back. But the response was generally the same: "We don't need the cars. You asked for them. Now they're yours."

It took months for the Orlando branch to unload its excess vehicles, a costly mistake that essentially wiped out all profits earned during the tourist season. "Corporate kept reminding us, 'You may be near the airport, but don't forget about the home-city business,'" one branch manager recalled. "But we ignored this warning. The lesson we learned is that the home-city business is there all year and can be counted on. Business from tourists fluctuates greatly with the seasons and the economy."

The incident also served as a clear demonstration of why it's important not to sacrifice the potential for short-term easy money at the expense of the long-term viability of your business model.

"I used to get upset because Enterprise was so conservative," another manager says. "Before going into the water, we'd measure the depth, then we'd send people to walk in slowly and critique the terrain on the bottom to see how it dropped off before saying, 'Okay, you can go in now.' It used to really upset me when the company wouldn't move as fast as I wanted. But now I realize that this go-slow and careful approach was really right."

About the most adventurous Jack got was trying new endeavors within Enterprise's still-conservative business model. For instance, during the 1960s, he struck a deal to start a rental car operation with the old Famous Barr department store chain in St. Louis.

"I worked at Famous Barr Rent-A-Car one summer right after my freshman year of college," Andy recalls. "It was my worst summer ever because there was no activity. I found myself talking to the women who worked in the budget shoe department all day, which got me into trouble with the store manager. That venture just didn't pan out."

Another short-lived experiment included starting Access Rent-A-Car. Unlike Enterprise, this company was a "no-frills" operation that supplied used (instead of new) cars to customers and offered no pick-up or drop-off service.

"We realized that people weren't just looking for price," company president Don Ross says. "They wanted quality and service, too. The no-frills idea was mine, but it ultimately proved to be a bad move."

From that point on, the company concentrated exclusively on expanding its core service-based Enterprise-branded car rental business that had been demonstrated to work so well.

Have Patience in Difficult Times

Enterprise's most financially difficult period came in the early 1970s, just as the company was beginning phase one of its real growth spurt. The country was faced with high gas prices, an energy crisis, a glut of unwanted luxury cars, and a deep recession that began to drain the company's cash reserves. Jack was convinced the tide would turn, and he was proven right. As 1974 progressed, business began to improve. Surviving the tough economic times wasn't easy, though it made some advantages of Enterprise's business model clear.

People kept their cars longer in a recession, which hurt the leasing side of the business. But these older vehicles spent more time in the repair shop, increasing demand for replacement vehicles. In addition, when the economy is weak, folks tend to get damaged cars repaired instead of buying something new. That means they need a replacement vehicle for a longer period of time.

"We are able to provide them with that temporary transportation," Ross says. "By the same token, if they get into an accident when money is tight, they repair their cars instead of buying a new one."

Likewise, families planning a lengthy car trip might rent a vehicle instead of putting miles on their own set of wheels. All of this worked to Enterprise's advantage. And as word spread about how easy it was to do business with the company, more customers started showing up at Enterprise branches.

In 1976, the company's top managers, perhaps fifteen in all, met at the Clayton Inn just outside of St. Louis. It was here that Jack announced his plans for a fast-track national expansion. At the time, the company had fledgling operations in four states outside of Missouri—Florida, Georgia, Texas, and Kansas. The Enterprise model had proved successful in several markets, and the number of good managers in the system had increased due to the company's growth. All of them were now ready to move on to additional challenges. Given that the financial resources and people were available, it was time for the company to invest in this expansion both through acquisition and from starting new offices from scratch. Whereas Enterprise previously entered a new market with a single branch and waited for it to turn profitable before opening another, it was now possible for several locations to open almost simultaneously.

"We were feeling good about our abilities, and life was going quite well," Andy Taylor says.

Set the Right Structure

While Jack had confidence the company could expand beyond its fairly limited borders, much of the actual expansion occurred on Andy's watch.

By now it was obvious to all senior personnel that a transition at the top was in the works. Andy had been taking on more and more responsibilities as Jack gradually relinquished control. What seemed remarkable to many was the relative tranquillity of the shift, given how tumultuous the passing of the torch can sometimes be in family-owned businesses. There was one particular meeting shortly before Andy began to assume more of a leadership role that underscored the fact that he was really his own man—and not someone who merely did what Jack wanted.

Enterprise holds regular senior management meetings, where everyone is encouraged to speak freely, offer opinions, and argue their cases. It used to be that after an issue was discussed from all sides, Jack would render a final decision. At this particular meeting, however, Jack and Andy disagreed on the resolution. Jack attempted to pull rank. But, somewhat to Jack's surprise, Andy countered by reiterating his position.

"I saw Jack Taylor sit back in his seat, relax, and smile," one manager recalls. "I knew it wouldn't be long before the transition was official. It was just a very human moment where you could see the transition starting to happen."

While the company's relentless focus on customer service remained unchanged, Andy had ambitious plans for its expansion. He placed a greater emphasis on the company's rental business, which led to exponential results, with Enterprise doubling in size every two to three years. In May 1983, branch 100 opened. Two years later, as Andy assumed more responsibility with each passing month, there were 175 branches. By 1991, the year Andy became CEO, Enterprise had more than 1,000 offices—all of which were primarily rental locations.

"Jack's vision of how far the company could go was more conservative than mine," Andy says. "I really felt Enterprise could be very large. When we committed to going national, I really was convinced we could do it, although it wasn't easy. I'm a huge believer that if your business isn't growing, you can't hold it steady. You're either going up or you're going down. To be honest, I'm not sure I ever imagined we'd be as big as we are. It really speaks to the effectiveness of the culture, the business model, and our people."

"I think it was a bit overwhelming for Dad to see the business grow as it did," observes Jack's daughter, Jo Ann Taylor Kindle. "When Dad was CEO, the company was small enough that he came to know everybody personally. As it got bigger, it was hard for him to accept that he didn't know everyone. He liked dealing with people on a one-on-one basis."

"I have to give my father a lot of credit, though, because as the business got bigger, he stayed the course and constantly reinvested in it," Andy adds. "Even today, we have consistently shown a willingness to make sure our branches have the capital needed to succeed, and we're willing to invest in the business to keep Enterprise a world-class company."

Up through the early 1990s, Enterprise funded all of its growth both through profits and by taking out loans—primarily from banks and automaker financing divisions, such as General Motors Acceptance Corporation and Ford Motor Credit. As the company grew, it expanded into bank syndication financing, in essence obtaining large lines of credit from a number of financial institutions that could be tapped as needed. Now much of Enterprise's growth is funded through private placements—specifically, bonds sold to major institutions. Given that Enterprise has an A– investment-grade rating from Standard & Poor's, the strongest in the industry, it is able to secure financing at extremely attractive rates—a powerful competitive advantage. Investors are particularly encouraged by Enterprise's long record of profitability, the fact that there have been only two CEOs in the company's fifty-year history, and its deep management bench, which consists of many top executives in their mid-forties who have been with the company for more than twenty years. In making sure there's always enough money available to fund future growth, the company's treasurer focuses on three primary areas: liquidity, flexibility, and cost. Liquidity refers to always having ready access to capital, flexibility means being able to take debt levels up or down as needed, and attention to cost translates into not paying more for the money than necessary.

Keep Growth Under Control

Although it all turned out well in the end, Andy admits that the company's confidence caused it to overexpand in the early 1980s. "We were growing revenues more than 30 percent a year and sometimes got a little ahead of ourselves," he says. "We put some people into positions where they couldn't succeed and opened branches in the wrong places. We also had a learning curve as we moved into different areas. For instance, we didn't understand that you can rent a car every day in the winter and summer in Denver, but your business really slows down in the fall and spring. That cost us a lot of money until we figured out how to properly cycle our fleet."

The overwhelming growth caused Enterprise to temporarily take its eye off the ball in the midst of this rapid expansion. As this happened, some smaller competitors tried moving in on the company's home-city territory, including Agency, Action, and Snappy Rent-A-Car.

"They saw what we were doing and tried to replicate our model," Andy says. "The biggest difference was they wanted to get rich fast, take the company public, and have a big payday. Our family-owned structure allowed us to take a long-term view of serving the customer first. I made sure I had enough financing in place that when our operators called and said they needed additional cars, we always had money for that."

Fortunately for Enterprise, shorter-term goals ultimately put many of these other competitors out of business or forced them to be acquired by one of the larger players.

"I think the biggest lesson we learned in the 1980s is that it's all about people," Andy reflects. "If you have any doubt about someone being able to manage or run one of your operations, don't put them in that position. More important, never lose sight of your core competencies."

Exploit Clearly Defined Niches

On top of the other growing pains, differences and competitiveness between the leasing and rental sides of Enterprise's business also initially created some small culture clashes. Prior to the huge rental spurt, all company general managers were required to have some leasing experience, which took a more sophisticated understanding of financing. This wasn't necessary on the more hands-on and physically active rental side, where a number of excellent rental managers had no interest whatsoever in leasing. At the same time, the company increasingly opened locations without leasing operations. Eventually Enterprise did away with the leasing requirement for its general managers, at which time the pool of available talent to drive the company's expansion overflowed.

There was no denying that leasing was, at best, holding steady as the rental car business exploded. By the time Enterprise got up to about 30,000 leases, car manufacturers were already heavily involved in leasing, as well. You could now lease a vehicle at almost any dealership. From the automaker's perspective, leases gave dealers a chance to sell customers another vehicle every few years, since terms tended to be fairly short. More important, it let manufacturers retain control of the resale market, while offering rock-bottom leasing rates through their financial arms at terms Enterprise couldn't match. Leasing was becoming a commodity business with no focus on service.

The eclipse of Enterprise's leasing division by rental and outside competition also meant that this business area was no longer seen as the only career path at Enterprise. The rental business had really arrived. So, in 1990, the company tasked a committee to look at the leasing market to help chart Enterprise's future direction—if any—in this area.

In a meeting convened by Andy Taylor, managers were divided over which way to go. They agreed to take a strategic look at the vehicle leasing industry and identify areas that meshed well with Enterprise's strengths. Independent companies routinely provide businesses with this kind of help, offering objective analysis and strategic plans. But one of the hallmarks of Enterprise's success is its "do-it-yourself" confidence and policies. A committee, more properly a team, of general managers and corporate vice presidents was created and given carte blanche to study the situation and make recommendations. The company also hired one key outsider to provide an objective perspective.

They started by talking to existing customers, initiating discussions with people throughout the industry, and chatting with the company's own employees about their thoughts on where the opportunities were and what they wanted to do. The committee's report laid out the situation: Auto manufacturers were creating a commodity business at the bottom end of the market, giving competitors little ability to differentiate themselves. At the top end, financial companies leased large fleets of vehicles to major national companies—the Avons, Frito-Lays, and Pepsis of the world. Enterprise had been involved in fleet services since 1976, when it began managing mid- to large-sized fleets for clients like ITT and Anheuser-Busch. A form of asset management, the services included providing advice on minimizing acquisition and holding costs, and an automated system that enabled customers to communicate with fleet services by green-screen monitors and modems.

It was concluded that neither the retail customer nor the large commercial market offered much opportunity for Enterprise. But in the middle was a segment of small to mid-sized businesses with fleets of 15 to 125 vehicles. For many of these companies, a leased fleet could make sense. For them, customer service mattered, and no one was specifically targeting this marketplace.

The committee developed a business plan to exploit this mid-tier market, and set up a career path for employees to enter and advance within the division. Meanwhile, the information technology department created software to track maintenance needs, monitor insurance and risk management, and even help automate the fleet lease sales process. The plan reenergized corporate support for Enterprise's leasing division. By focusing on this niche part of the fleet services market, the company went from a plateau of 30,000 leased vehicles in the 1980s to 170,000 vehicles and continued strong growth today. The company officially renamed its leasing operations Enterprise Fleet Services in 1993.

At the same time, by staying attuned to new opportunities, Enterprise started a commercial truck rental division in 1999. Unlike most competitors, the company chose not to compete with the do-it-yourself market Ryder and U-Haul made popular. After studying the landscape, Enterprise instead saw an opportunity to provide daily, weekly, and monthly rentals—from cargo vans to twenty-six-foot box trucks—to commercial fleet operators.

Liability laws covering trucks differ from state to state, in some cases depending on whether the truck is a commercial or retail rental. That's why Enterprise began its truck rental business in states with laws most favorable to such commercial rentals. The company won't shy away from tougher markets, but it decided to learn the business in areas offering the fewest impediments to success. The first two years were spent basically experimenting in selected markets. The company has slowly been expanding into more areas, refining the model, and expanding the rollout. In a sign of how impressively the business is accelerating, Enterprise had 5,900 trucks in service in October 2004. By the following summer, that number had jumped to 8,000, and it now stands in excess of 10,000. At least half of the market in the United States remains untapped. Company officers admit they have the financial muscle to grow more quickly, but they want to use the expansion of this business to reward those working their way up in the company instead of bringing in managers from the outside to develop the business as fast as possible.

"There's no rush, since we believe the market will still be there two or three years from now," notes Ross. "We want to make sure we're doing the right thing for our people by creating new opportunities for them. We don't want to just throw another business at our groups that they are not ready for, since this could hurt their overall performance and affect their careers. If we were to expand into every market right away, we'd have to do it in a way that would not meet our standards."

"If someone raises their hand and says they want to add another business, they must first be managing other divisions in their group well," adds Andy Taylor. "You must have the customer and employee satisfaction, and be growing your other divisions properly, before taking something else on. Expanding too fast can negatively impact customer satisfaction, which spreads everywhere and causes reputation problems."

Expanding to Airports

As you know, Enterprise built its business by avoiding the more crowded airport market. Not only was it already dominated by many major national brands, it was also an expensive operating environment. As local governments sought new ways to increase revenues, they began levying surcharges on rental car transactions conducted at the airport, which quickly began to add up. Perhaps more important, with its emphasis on the speed of transactions, airports didn't give Enterprise the opportunity to really showcase its customer service skills. Still, there was no denying the huge size of this market, and given the autonomy Enterprise general managers have, some decided to open new locations near select terminals. At the same time, as the company's name recognition grew, more customers started inquiring about whether Enterprise offered airport rentals.

"The people that rented from us in the local market said, 'Why can't I rent from you guys when I fly to see my mom in Chicago? Don't you have an office nearby?'" says one manager. "Often we did, but the branch really wasn't an airport office per se."

Since there was no standard policy about whether airports could be serviced, Enterprise employees were generally willing to pick up airport customers in regular vehicles at baggage claim, just as they long had at body shops and homes. However, if customers had to travel more than ten minutes to get a car, they likely wouldn't be satisfied by the experience. They had already been on a long plane ride, after all, and didn't want to wait another hour to get their rental car. At the same time, airport authorities began extending those extra surcharges to cover nearby rental locations that served local airports, making such Enterprise branches de facto airport offices whether the company intended it or not. Nevertheless, Andy and Jack remained reluctant to make a major commitment to the airport market, particularly because they weren't sure such locations could deliver on the high level of customer satisfaction on which the company was built. This was based, in large part, on the fact that near-airport locations often had ESQi scores that weren't up to company standards.

Furthermore, airport locations had a different model than the home-city market. The shorter rental cycles required a new kind of fleet planning and altered way of thinking. Yet research showed there was an opportunity for the company in the airport market, especially by servicing customers from nearby off-site locations. Enterprise decided that if it was going to operate at airports, it didn't want to be a "me too" brand. Unless it could deliver the same completely satisfying experience customers at its home-city branches received, the company wanted to stay out of the airport business altogether. After more studies and discussions in the early 1990s, Enterprise decided to dip its toes into this market. But what was the best location for an initial test site?

In 1995, Denver opened the first major new airport in America in more than thirty years. It was built twenty-four miles east of the city center on a flat prairie with almost nothing around it.

Since there was no off-site location close enough to open a branch, Enterprise decided to take space at the airport itself and use this as a test facility to identify and refine best practices, hoping to keep the experiment under the radar. The company discovered that the simple things, which made a difference in city branches, worked at the airport, too. Employees helped customers with their baggage, made sure they knew how to operate the vehicle, asked whether the vehicle was suitable, and closed the rental by finding out what could have been done better.

"The first big 'ah-ha' moment was when we realized how much customers appreciated our branded service," says one manager involved in the airport expansion program, "because the initial perception is that the airport rental is all about speed. Yes, you need to be quick, but you need that personal touch, too. Frankly, this somewhat surprised us at first."

The next major realization that this could work came in 1998. Enterprise received a call from J.D. Power and Associates saying it had won first place in the consulting group's annual survey of customer service levels provided by retail companies operating on or near airports. "Believe it or not, we didn't have your name on the survey," Enterprise executives were told, "but customers wrote your name in because of the good service they received."

Though it was flattered, Enterprise wasn't ready to be acknowledged for serving the airport market yet, since the endeavor was still in the experimental stage.

"We said, 'Can we get back to you on this, because we're not sure we want to tell the world we're an airport rent-a-car company?'" Ross reveals. "Frankly, we weren't certain we had this market all figured out yet." Ultimately, Enterprise declined the award that year.

Instead, the company set up more internal controls for this new division. Among other things, Enterprise required that any airport branch be located within fifteen minutes of the airport and facing in the direction of downtown, making it easier for travelers unfamiliar with the area to get where they needed to go.

By 1999, Enterprise was ready to make a formal entry into the airport market, unveiling an ambitious expansion plan. Two to three on-site airport locations were added monthly over the next seven years, a pace that continues today. The company could have grown the segment faster, but it was concerned about maintaining quality control. As part of its growth strategy, Enterprise started courting travel agents to get them more familiar with the company. After instituting these new policies, Enterprise let J.D. Power and Associates know that it was now in contention for the service award. That same year, it tied Hertz for first place and had the top honor for five of the next six years.

As other airport car rental companies have seen their market shares shrink, especially in the aftermath of 9/11, Enterprise's airport business has taken off, a testament to its way of doing business. It also serves as confirmation that entering the market slowly and deliberately was the right course of action.

Growing Internationally

No matter how large or well-oiled your organization, if you want to expand it into new areas, you must have the ability to adapt. In new areas and countries, conditions can be markedly different. Enterprise's experience with its overseas expansion effort underscores this point. The company's move into Canada in the early 1990s was relatively seamless, because the market is so similar to that of the United States. The company's Canadian business is flourishing, with more than 2,600 employees (nearly all Canadian citizens) operating 380 branches and some 30,000 cars.

In three of the last four years, Enterprise Canada has been voted one of the 50 best employers by the *Globe and Mail* newspaper.

When Enterprise tried to establish a foothold in Europe in 1994, however, things were not as easy at first. Enterprise had to adapt its way of doing business to local customs and cultures.

First up, Enterprise targeted the United Kingdom as the home of its first European office. Before opening an office there, the company attended job fairs at British universities to recruit prospective employees. Experts told Enterprise that Europeans didn't care as much about customer service as Americans. They also warned that Enterprise's merit- and performance-based pay system wouldn't fly in Europe. But the reality was far different. Enterprise found that people were just as interested in good service in Europe as they were everywhere else. After all, good customer service knows no boundaries. It was just that they had never been exposed to it in the rental car industry before. And, indeed, there was a significant pool of job candidates intrigued by Enterprise's unique compensation structure.

The first challenge the company faced was building awareness of the Enterprise brand in Europe. The business landscape for the rental car industry was completely different. The insurance replacement business didn't exist in the same fashion as in the United States.

In the United Kingdom, body shops typically kept loaner vehicles for their customers, and the cost of the rental was built into the price of the repair. The insurance companies, and certainly the body shops, saw no reason to change the way they did business. As a result, success didn't come quickly. Losses amounted to some $2 million during Enterprise's first two years of operation, and some of its bright management trainees left after early hopes of success failed to materialize. Enterprise decided that major changes were required in order to thrive in the U.K. It relocated five branches and dug into the corporate treasury to open fifteen more offices in southeast England to ensure that it could adequately service potential business.

Enterprise had to determine which cultural differences it had to adapt to while retaining those core policies that kept the company true to its values. For example, managers taught new hires to shake the hands of all customers. The British said this approach simply wouldn't work in the United Kingdom. "That's not what we do," some insisted. "Shaking hands is an American thing, and it won't go over here."

When some of Enterprise's new hires returned to England after undergoing training in the United States, one manager asked how many people shook their hands in the United Kingdom on a daily basis. "It only happens at Enterprise," one answered. The manager replied, "See? It's not an *American* thing. It's an *Enterprise* thing. The gesture creates a personal connection with your customer." Not surprisingly, the handshake stayed and remains a differentiating factor.

Although some rental car companies in the United Kingdom dropped off cars for customers, no one else provided anything close to Enterprise's "pick-up" service, which proved popular. It was far more accepted because of the drawbacks to the traditional car rental delivery service in the U.K., in which disputes arose when customers claimed damage occurred to cars before they took possession of them. When you added in parking tickets, the amount of fuel used, and mileage charges—which were calculated after the car was dropped off—customers had a litany of potential problems and complaints against these legacy rental companies.

In Europe, conditions are different from country to country. As a result, Enterprise had to address the needs of each market individually. The Republic of Ireland, for instance, was much more conservative than the United Kingdom and less willing to try new approaches in the insurance market.

The company's fleets had to be rethought for the European market, too. Enterprise learned, for instance, that Germans like to rent and drive German cars. Color preferences are also different. White is the most popular color in the American fleet; customers in the United Kingdom prefer silver, and blue is more popular than red. It proved to be an expensive lesson, as rates for white and foreign-built cars had to be dropped in order to keep them rented. Customers wanted diesel-operated vehicles as well, which Enterprise didn't offer when it first opened in Europe.

Today, though corporate business still dominates Enterprise's European operation, insurance replacement rentals comprise an increasing portion of revenues in Ireland and the United Kingdom. This market is growing quickly in Germany as well. But the company continues to evolve its European operations to deal with the many differences among individual countries. ARMS, the automated system that helps manage insurance replacement cars in the United States, required significant modifications to meet the needs of the European market, and the company is still wrestling with the challenge of making it useful there.

The potential for expansion in a competitive environment can also create problems. Enterprise continues to see lots of room for growth in Europe, but so do other major American-based rental car companies. As a result, Enterprise has to balance growing quickly in order to establish a market position with the need to maintain the quality service that distinguishes the company. So far, Enterprise's strategy appears to be working well.

"Our European fleet surpassed the 40,000-car mark in late 2005, and we topped 4,600 people and more than 450 locations," notes Andy Taylor. "It took us 25 years in the United States to accomplish what we have done in 10 years in Europe. We now operate successfully in four nations outside of the United States."

Diversify into Areas in Line with Your Core Competencies

In the company's early days, Jack Taylor's wife looked forward to having a cup of coffee in the morning when the family went on vacations together. As a result, he'd often find himself calling room service or walking down to the motel diner to grab a cup for her.

In the early 1970s, Jack got to know the owners of Keefe Coffee, a St. Louis-based company that offered packets of in-room instant coffee for hotels and motels. Keefe had annual sales of about $250,000, mostly to small motels across the country. When Keefe approached Jack about buying the company, he was intrigued. If the automobile business became unreliable, he thought, it might make sense to hedge his bets by diversifying into other areas.

Some at Enterprise questioned the wisdom of getting into the coffee business—company accountants among them. But going on his gut instinct, Jack decided to buy Keefe in 1974 and put Andy in charge of running it. It was the first Enterprise-related business Andy headed, and it marked the company's initial foray into diversifying outside of the core car rental industry. After analyzing the market, Andy concluded that Keefe had huge potential, especially if it could provide excellent customer service to motel proprietors, something Enterprise and its people understood how to do well.

Keefe became the first in a series of businesses the Taylors would go on to purchase through a separate operating division, formerly known as the Enterprise Capital Group (ECG). It was charged with acquiring and managing small, diversified companies with significant growth potential. But ECG's next venture didn't pan out. It would be a humbling lesson.

In 1977, the company heard about a business called Mexican Inn Chili Products. It was owned by a friend of Doug Brown, one of Enterprise's general managers, and supplied Mexican food to local institutional markets. "We figured we could take these products and sell them through retail chains, not just to schools and other places like that," Andy Taylor says. "We bought the company for around $400,000, which was a lot of money back then." But it was quickly apparent that some realities of the business were masked by the seeming synergies. First, both the retail and institutional food products were sold to grocery stores, schools, and restaurants by outside brokers, rather than directly to the end consumer. As a result, ECG had no opportunity to forge personal relationships and set itself apart by delivering quality customer service. Moreover, Mexican Inn's frozen meals were a commodity. Buyers responded primarily to price. They didn't care what level of service was provided as long as shipments were on time and inexpensive. And operating in the crowded retail space was costly. ECG spent considerable time and resources trying to make Mexican Inn successful. In the end, Andy decided to concede defeat and closed the business down.

"The first loss is the best loss," he told Jack. "We missed the opportunity to cut our losses early, and now is the time to do it."

Jack agreed. The effort was an expensive failure, one of few in the company's history. But it provided a valuable demonstration of how *not* to diversify in the future.

"In hindsight, the business was totally different from the way we had succeeded," Andy explains. "We were not dealing directly with the consumer. Our big advantage is we have great people and customers really like us. In this case, our people never saw the customers, and we could not leverage any of our skills back into that business. We also brought in outsiders to run the company, and that did not work because there was a culture clash."

From that point on, the Taylors were careful to see that every future business they bought outside of the car rental industry was built on customer contact and service—in other words, the same model the original company was built on. The Mexican Inn debacle begat a rallying cry that Andy has used ever since when managers present him with a new business opportunity to evaluate: "Don't give me a Mexican Inn!"

In 1999, ECG was spun off into a separate company owned by the Taylor family called The Centric Group. Centric has since put together a collection of seemingly disparate businesses, all of which offer products built upon taking good care of customers. Today, Centric has some 1,700 employees and revenues of more than $600 million a year. Its chief executive officer is Doug Albrecht, who started out at Enterprise Rent-A-Car before being hired as Keefe Coffee's first full-time employee in 1974. It is operated on a business model similar to Enterprise's, with many employees being compensated based partly on bottom-line results. Furthermore, Centric seeks niches where it can stand out from the rest of the crowded marketplace.

"In all of these businesses, we're dealing with the customer. In addition, our people are ingrained in our culture and know our values, they understand that customer satisfaction and being a good teammate are the first two tenets of our business, they have an interest in growing the company, they are promoted based on customer satisfaction, and they realize that we take a long-term view concerning profitability," Andy notes.

Centric remains heavily involved in the hospitality business through what is now known as the Keefe Group. Keefe's offerings include thousands of commissary and lodging items, such as food, clothing, electronics, and personal-care products. Its most popular products, beyond coffee, include clock radios with big numbers on the digital display that are easier to see in the dark, along with energy-efficient in-room irons and hair dryers.

Centric has also become a major supplier to another kind of lodging facility: prisons. Centric has businesses that sell products to prison commissaries. The items are redesigned or specifically altered for this market. Take the snacks inmates buy through vending machines. The food served in correctional institutions tends to be bland, though research shows many inmates want spicier options. As a result, Centric reformulates its snack foods to make them spicier or sweeter. Products like mouthwash are reformulated to remove alcohol from the ingredients, or repackaged to make single-serve containers, an important consideration for that niche market. Centric even operates the commissary altogether in some correctional institutions.

Customer service is important in the correctional market, especially given the restive nature of the population being served. When a prison in Jackson, Michigan, called one day in a near panic because the facility ran out of coffee, a Centric manager drove overnight to deliver new supplies. Prison officials had no idea what would happen if inmates awoke to find there was no coffee. The Centric team made sure they didn't have to find out.

Centric felt that low-cost footwear would do well in the correctional facility marketplace, as well as in the general market. After cutting its teeth in this space by distributing inexpensive athletic shoes, the company ultimately purchased the manufacturing and marketing rights for Riddell footwear. Now it has expanded into manufacturing luggage by licensing the names of premier companies, such as Swiss Army and Callaway Golf, to brand high-quality products ranging from briefcases to golf bags. Centric also owns Betallic, a company that makes Mylar balloons and gift boxes for floral displays and welcome packages.

While these businesses seem to have little in common, the focus on differentiating its products in the marketplace, and providing outstanding service to customers, fits with Enterprise's overall operating philosophy and proves that "The Enterprise Way" can effectively be applied to almost any industry, even one as mundane as making balloons.

Running a Successful Business Is a Marathon, Not a 100-Yard Dash

Above all, when it comes to growth, Enterprise believes in running its business like a marathon, not a 100-yard dash. "All businesses experience ups and downs," Andy Taylor says. "Those that focus on the long term, instead of temporary setbacks, will be more successful in the end."

While admiring how far Enterprise has come, posting 20.5 percent compound annual growth for the last twenty-five years, Andy is careful to point out that this growth didn't come overnight. "No matter how smart or talented you are, you have to put in the work," he adds. "You must keep yourself educated about your market, the competition, and your own capabilities. Most important, you must be surrounded by good people."

Company president Don Ross refers to Enterprise's growth strategy as being "thoughtful" and "balanced."

"We like to grow lockstep with our employees, to make sure we're doing the right thing," Ross says. "It's important to be thoughtful about our next steps. It's part of our culture. Rather than just running out there and taking the chance of failing, we say, 'Let's go slow and make sure we're getting it right.'"

Enterprise doesn't focus on what's happening with its operations over the next week or month. Instead, it looks out over the coming five years. In preparing this forecast, the challenges of today are weighed against the future direction the company intends to move in. The forecast is updated every twelve to eighteen months and is overseen by a strategy committee that meets at least four times a year, depending on industry conditions. For instance, the recent sale of a major rental car company sparked a flurry of impromptu discussions as the committee contemplated what this ownership change might portend for the industry and the competitive landscape, along with what moves Enterprise should make to stay ahead of these eventualities.

What's more, Enterprise has discovered that, while it is always open to new ideas and approaches, it is essential that any endeavor stick to the company's central operating principles.

"We are very strategic and want to understand what we do well and what segment of the business we can service best," says chief operating officer Pam Nicholson. "In rental, we found our niche in the insurance replacement business and evolved into a much larger business based on our ability to listen to, and please, our customers. We don't want to lose focus. Even now as we move into the airport market, we have zeroed in on that segment of airport travelers that we feel we can service best."

This doesn't mean that Enterprise won't keep targeting new segments, such as the general aviation market, which has been a particular priority of late. As part of its corporate marketing effort, Enterprise is one of a few car rental companies reaching out to private pilots, fixed-base operators, and other segments of the aviation industry, especially those operating at the fast-growing smaller regional airports that might not have any other car rental options on site.

"People are always coming to us, both internally and from the outside, with business ideas they think we should fund," Andy Taylor says. "We usually say 'no.' We have to be careful to stay focused on those businesses we can really service well. To date, we've made a decision to stick to our 'organic growth' model. We've decided against growing by acquisition. To this day, when we enter a new market or launch a new line of business, we take a 'greenfield' approach and build it from scratch. That's the only way to ensure that our new ventures remain true to Enterprise's culture and heritage."

While Andy continues to lead the company's growth efforts, Jack remains "actively interested" in the businesses, always wanting to hear about what's going on.

"He really helps to keep the culture together here," Andy says. "Jack's always asking, 'Are we treating our employees well? Are customers happy?' In the end, those are the key questions, and answering them well will allow us to continue to prosper and build a sustainable business over the next fifty years and beyond."

THE ENTERPRISE WAY

1. Take a cautious and thoughtful approach to growing your business.
2. Limit your risk. One way to reduce risk when opening a new office is by asking for a "JCT Clause," as Enterprise puts it. This provision, added to some long-term leases, allows the company to get out of its lease with ninety days' notice and the payment of three additional months of rent.

3. Avoid sacrificing the potential for easy short-term money at the expense of the long-term viability of your business.

4. Every company goes through tough economic times. Use such periods to reinforce the advantages you bring to the marketplace, while putting an even greater emphasis on improving operations so you can stand strong when the tide turns.

5. Have the right team and systems in place before embarking on a major expansion.

6. It's all about people. If you have any doubt about whether someone can run one of your operations, don't put them in that position in the first place.

7. Keep investing in your business in order to make it a world-class operation.

8. Understand that business cycles differ from city to city. For instance, Enterprise found out the hard way that it's hard to rent cars in Denver during the fall and spring, which is nearly the opposite of the cycle in Florida.

9. As you grow, never lose sight of your company's core competencies.

10. Have ready access to capital in order to fund your growth, paying attention to three crucial elements of financing: liquidity, flexibility, and cost.

11. When competitors start moving into your territory, figure out new ways to stand apart. (As one example, when dealerships began offering car leases of their own, Enterprise turned its attention to the mid-tier fleet services market that was otherwise being ignored.)

12. If you choose to diversify your business into unrelated

areas, do so only if these operations mesh well with your core strengths. If your business is built on offering excellent customer service, for instance, don't buy a company that never deals directly with the end-use customer.

13. Just because you have the money to do so doesn't mean you must expand operations as fast as possible. Do it only when you're ready and have the right people and systems in place.

14. When embarking on new business ventures, start small by testing. That way you can further refine what works best, or decide to cut your losses if things don't go as planned.

15. Once you begin moving into international markets, be sensitive to local customs and cultures—and how they will impact your business.

16. Companies that focus on the long term—and run a marathon instead of the 100-yard dash—will enjoy the greatest successes. Look out over the next five years, not the coming weeks and months.

17. Don't lose focus on what you do best. Even as you get bigger, keep zeroing in on your core customers.

Live Your Core Values

IN THEIR BESTSELLING business book *Built to Last*, authors James Collins and Jerry Porras assert that one of the primary traits found among the world's most successful companies is a steadfast adherence to a group of core values unique to their individual culture. Taking it a bit further, General Electric chairman and chief executive officer Jeffrey Immelt has said, "To earn trust, you must have values. Values give you a rock-solid sense of who you are, what you believe in, which side you're on." And, according to Enterprise CEO Andy Taylor, "Core values are like a rallying point for the organization. If you choose them wisely and thoughtfully in the context of all your stakeholders, it will protect your reputation, make your employees feel good about you and your organization, and give customers a good feeling about your company."

Core values, in essence, are the essential and enduring guiding principles of an organization that impact how everyone in the company thinks and acts. They are fundamental guideposts that transcend economic cycles, management changes, technological advancements, and the ever-fluctuating marketplace. They represent the beliefs and ideals everyone in the organization holds dear. Often, rather than being conscientiously created, core values emerge out of the lessons and examples handed down by the company's founder. And while they may evolve over time, a company's core values should remain largely unchanged, regardless of which new business directions a company may pursue or what opportunities may emerge in the future. That's because each strategic decision should circle back to whether it fits in with the company's core values.

It's important not to confuse core values with slogans or catchphrases. Although sometimes related, slogans can be hollow and emanate from the marketing department rather than long-ingrained cultural beliefs. Unlike ad campaigns, core values begin and end right at the heart of a company. They guide every move, and they are the primary rallying point that each employee must get behind to ensure the organization's longevity.

"It's sort of like how every company says they're into customer satisfaction," Andy Taylor observes. "While they may be, and perhaps they even measure it, they don't really live it. By having core values and making sure you stand behind them, you prove to people that you live these beliefs and, in turn, become a special place. There is an upside for having businesses under attack these days. By having a list of core values, and sticking to them, you are given an opportunity to distance yourself from everyone else."

Codify Your Beliefs

Enterprise's core values started to form when Jack Taylor leased his first car back in 1957. He lived and breathed them every day. When Enterprise was smaller, most employees knew Jack personally and were well aware of what he stood for, even though the company's values weren't set forth in a formal document.

"When I started here, we could sit around a table with Jack and talk about what needed to be done," recalls company president Don Ross.

"Even when I came on board in the 1970s and through the 1980s, most employees at some point had a chance to meet Jack or me and get a firsthand sense of who we are and how we do business," adds Andy Taylor.

But as the company grew and got older, many of the company's leaders in the field weren't lucky enough to have experienced this one-on-one interaction with Jack. By the 1990s, the company was well into its second and third generation of leaders. While they had long been taught about what Jack and Enterprise stood for, and may have even had the chance to shake hands with the man himself at some point, executives wanted to solidify the company's cultural beliefs in a way that wouldn't somehow get lost in translation.

In 2002, Enterprise decided to codify its core values by writing them down and ensuring that they were carefully articulated to every employee in the organization. They are referred to as Enterprise's "founding" values, because they capture the beliefs of company founder Jack Taylor.

"We didn't just sit down and jot a list of values on a piece of paper," Andy Taylor points out. "These are principles we had been talking about since the company's founding. They are the values the Taylor family—and the Enterprise family—have believed in and lived for decades. We simply decided to present them in a more formal way."

Having them in writing helps to make sure the values get clearly articulated to the most recently hired person and those at all levels of the company.

"We don't just write them down, we talk about them all the time and at every training session," Andy says. "Only great companies clearly and consistently communicate their values to employees and build them into the fabric of the organization. We consider Enterprise to be a great company, so it only makes sense for us to ask employees to honor these values on a regular basis."

A few years ago, Enterprise placed its eight founding values on a small plastic card, the size of a business card, that every employee can keep in their pockets at all times. The company's reputation, fleet size, and workforce had exploded, and Enterprise decided that putting its values in such a readily accessible format would help to make these operating principles more fully understood and embraced by everyone, including customers. The card serves as a constant reminder of the mission they are on and the duty each is charged with upholding every day.

But there were also other motivations for putting these values down in writing.

"To be honest, we had some isolated instances in the late 1990s where some customers and employees weren't being treated fairly. In some cases, we faced lawsuits over the inappropriate business practices that occurred within a handful of our groups. That greatly troubled Jack and me," Andy Taylor admits. "This cost the company money and, more important, damaged Enterprise's good name. It also went against everything we believe in. When we all operate from the same set of founding values, our odds of continued success increase a hundredfold."

Enterprise goes a step further by rewarding those groups that best exemplify each of these values through what is known as the Jack Taylor Founding Values Award. "It doesn't require having the best ESQi or operating profit to win one," observes Ross. "You just have to show that you're doing a good job of living these values. We want to drive home that this is something you should always think about. It's about staying close to our roots and reminding people of what we stand for."

Winning this honor is a big deal at Enterprise.

"Awards are huge here—even bigger than a paycheck," Nicholson says. "People say, 'Keep the money and give me the award,' which around here we call 'the wood.' We're very big on recognition, and awards generally lead to promotions."

Enterprise refers to its eight founding values as "the values that define us and drive us." What are they?

1. Our brand is the most valuable thing we own.
2. Personal honesty and integrity are the foundation of our success.
3. Customer service is our way of life.
4. Enterprise is a fun and friendly place, where teamwork rules.
5. We work hard . . . and we reward hard work.
6. Great things happen when we listen . . . to our customers and to one another.
7. We strengthen our communities one neighborhood at a time.
8. Our doors are open.

As you can see, while clearly unique to Enterprise, these values reflect a belief system beneficial to organizations of all types. Throughout the rest of this chapter, we'll examine each core value individually, show you how Enterprise lives every one on a daily basis, and help you discover how to incorporate a similar list of guiding principles into your own organization.

Protect Your Brand

A company's brand is its most important possession. When a brand is tarnished, it can quickly destroy a company and everything it has worked so hard to build.

"Enterprise became a world-class company one handshake and promise at a time," says Andy Taylor. "Our company is only as strong as the reputation that each employee maintains in the minds of our customers, potential customers, and employees."

"One way we protect the brand is by measuring customer service," Nicholson adds.

"In my mind, the Enterprise brand stands for high quality, high service, and high values," says Ross.

Keeping the brand strong takes the efforts and dedication of everyone in the organization.

"We also want people to be able to recognize us, which is yet another part of our branding," says Nicholson. "That's why our signs and branches all look a certain way. People need to know they're coming into an Enterprise office wherever in the world they may be, and that they will be treated very well when they do."

"I want our employees to think of the Enterprise brand name as being something they own and have a responsibility to grow, strengthen, and protect," says Andy Taylor. "Our brand is our reputation. We need to protect it and make sure people know who we are and what we stand for."

Have Honesty and Integrity in All That You Do

"Honesty and integrity is something that's just so ingrained in our culture," says Nicholson. "I've been hearing this from the first day I started at the company. We give people a lot of autonomy and want them to feel ownership. But if we ever have a valid reason to question their integrity, they're gone. Honesty is everything."

Among the key tenets of Enterprise's training program is making it clear that employees are expected to take the high road and do what's right every time. This is especially crucial given that

Enterprise employees are allowed to operate so autonomously in the field. They are continually making decisions, without having to get approval from on high. The company insists that if employees keep these values in mind, they'll pretty much make the right decision every time. If not, they are expected to fess up right away. Lying about a problem is one of the quickest paths to termination at the company.

"We're all going to make mistakes along the way," says Nicholson. "Just don't lie about it and try to cover it up. That's the worst thing you could ever do."

Ross got a close-up look at the importance of this core value—and how serious the company was about it—back in his days as a general manager in Kansas City. "Every Tuesday, I'd get a call from Jack and our then-CFO, Warren Knapp, to discuss business and what happened during the prior week," he says. "One day they called and wanted to talk about a sale I made for a Suburban, which was a fairly expensive car even in those days."

Jack told Ross he was trying to figure out how he came to his reported profit figure. Ross pulled the file to find out.

"I started running the numbers on my adding machine, and I said, 'Oh my gosh. I can see what I did here,'" Ross says.

"What do you mean?" Jack replied.

"I calculated the interest cost, but I forgot to add it in. So we don't really have any profit at all in this deal."

"Okay," Jack replied.

"What do you want me to do?" Ross asked.

"I don't want you to do anything," Jack told him. "We sort of thought that's what happened but wanted to find out for sure."

Shortly after the conversation ended, Jack phoned Ross again to tell him how much he appreciated his honesty.

"We had a similar circumstance with someone else earlier today, and after an hour and a half, he finally owned up," Jack told Ross. "You made an honest mistake, and your honesty is what we're looking for. That's the kind of confidence I want to have with you, that you'll be honest with me regarding the good and bad."

This sent a powerful message to Ross, one he has never forgotten.

"You can say it all, but when you have an opportunity to demonstrate a moment of truth like that, it's very powerful," Ross says. "When it starts at the top, it sort of migrates its way through the rest of the organization. Is it perfect here? No. But the more we reinforce it, and continue to talk about this as a core value, the greater the likelihood that it will continue to be enforced."

To continue on its growth track, Andy Taylor insists that the company will settle for nothing less than honesty and integrity from everyone in the organization, starting with him.

"When you are an officer of this business, the requirements for honesty and integrity are even higher than for the typical employee," he says. "If you are going to be paid the most, and if you have been here the longest, the bar needs to be set higher. It's called leadership, and it goes back to the brand. The most important thing we own, besides the relationship with our customers and employees, is our brand and reputation. I'm a real stickler on that."

Enterprise knows that much of its success is due to the realization that it's not just a car company. Its business is maintaining relationships with its many customers and employees.

"That's why it's critical for each of us to have an unwavering commitment to the highest ethical standards," Andy Taylor insists. "The only way to build healthy, long-term relationships is to treat people fairly. We must meet the needs of our customers and earn their trust. If employees fail in these areas, it chips away at our good name, and that's not acceptable."

Make Customer Service a
Way of Life

Andy Taylor likes to say that delivering excellent customer service comes as easily to Enterprise employees as breathing. "Throughout our history, customers have been drawn to us—and stayed with us—because we truly believe in and deliver courteous, personalized service," he says.

The company's sharp and consistent focus on customer service is an essential component of every aspect of its operations. It's the reason employees dress professionally, and it is the basis of whether or not someone gets promoted. It's also why each branch's ESQi score gets displayed right next to the profit numbers on monthly financial statements.

But there's another reason this value is so important.

"If you treat your customers right, they'll come back and tell other people about you," notes Nicholson. "That's really how we've grown. Our business used to come all from word-of-mouth referrals, so we counted on every customer telling the next person they saw or talked to."

While most companies claim to embrace this value, the vast majority fall short. What can businesses do to effectively beef up the level of customer service delivered by frontline employees?

"The first thing you have to do is start at the top," Ross insists. "Where is the CEO on this issue, and what is the CEO's commitment to improving customer service? You then move it through the next level of officers and come up with a measurable and achievable plan for getting those numbers up. Next, you start communicating the message of what needs to be done and how to do it. But if the people at the top are not committed, it's not going to happen."

Create a Fun and Friendly Place
Where Teamwork Rules

Whenever Jack Taylor meets a new employee, the first thing he asks is "Are you having fun?" It's a very sincere question. Enjoying what he did for a living was very important to Jack when he started Enterprise, especially given all he had been through in the war. The desire to create a culture that embraced this belief has never changed.

"I do believe that people do their work better if they enjoy it and are having fun," Andy Taylor says. "If they are having fun with their customers, their teammates are going to go home happier. They are going to wake up in the morning and say, 'I like going to work.'"

Given the hard work and long hours involved in renting cars, executives know that if their people aren't enjoying what they're doing, they will never last on the job. The concept of having fun, therefore, permeates the organization. And it's combined with a strong commitment to teamwork, which is critical given that Enterprise's business is all about managing the assets spread throughout its independently managed branch offices as effectively as possible.

"That means if my branch has too many cars and yours is running short, I'll loan you some cars and know I'll get them back when I need them," Ross says. "Our business model is fluid enough that people know they're all in this together. I might be a branch manager here today, but six months from now I could be over there. If I play well with my fellow peers, I am more likely to be viewed as a good leader and improve my chances of a promotion."

"When we expanded into Northern Ireland, Great Britain's Prince Andrew was on a world tour and came through St. Louis to thank us for the business," Andy Taylor recalls. "Our way of having fun was not for him to come sit in this office with me or meet him in private at a club. We told everyone he was coming and set up a stage downstairs so we could share him with our employees. More than 1,000 people showed up waving American and Union Jack flags. We put him on the stage next to my father, because they were both navy pilots. After the event, his staff told us it was the warmest welcome Prince Andrew ever had in his career. Our people went nuts, and it gave us huge credibility in their eyes."

Recognition is a big deal at Enterprise. It's also one of the ways the company instills the idea of having fun. "We have a lot of competitions, where one city will compete with another for customer satisfaction, profitability, or growth," Andy says. "If one group loses to another, they might cook the winner a steak dinner."

Such events are a way for Enterprise employees to build camaraderie and strengthen their ability to effectively work together as members of a unified team. At the same time, however, it's important to keep fun and forged friendships in check by never forgetting that business comes first.

"Enterprise has grown and prospered by attracting enthusiastic people who work and compete hard," says Andy. "We want our people to enjoy themselves. I want employees to wake up every morning excited about going to work for Enterprise, as I do."

Work Hard and Reward Hard Work

Succeeding at Enterprise requires a strong personal commitment.

"This is not an easy business," Andy Taylor admits. "Many times you are dealing with people who have had accidents, and they don't necessarily want to be talking with you. The hours are long, and working with the public—be it in America, Canada, or anywhere else—is not always easy. We've articulated this as a value because we want everyone who comes to work here to understand that."

In return for this hard work, Enterprise aptly rewards its employees personally, professionally, and financially. According to Andy Taylor, the core value of rewarding hard work reminds him of several rare qualities found at Enterprise, all of which open the door to opportunities unlike those found in most other organizations.

"For one thing, our company comes about as close as you can get to a true meritocracy," he points out. "Talent and productivity get rewarded. If you consistently do well, we'll compensate you for the results you generate. If you demonstrate an appetite for expanded responsibility, we'll do our best to give you all the growth opportunities you can handle."

Compensation for performance, recognition, and promotion from within all serve to reward hardworking employees. And it's also part of the two-way commitment the company makes with its team members.

"If you make this commitment to us and take care of our customers, we'll make a commitment to you," says Ross. "You'll know we won't go hire some gunslinger from the outside to come take over the corporate sales position in your area. We'll give you a shot at it if it's something you want. It is our way of rewarding you for your support."

Listen to Your Customers—and Each Other

Enterprise has succeeded by consistently doing some fairly simple things extremely well. Among them is listening.

"I've always been told that people should spend twice as much time listening as they do talking," says Andy Taylor. "That's why we have two ears and one mouth."

Listening is so important, he says, because that's how you uncover new opportunities to grow and more effectively operate your business.

"For instance, listening to his leasing customers convinced Jack there was a huge, untapped market for daily and weekly rentals," Andy says. "More recently, paying close attention to what our customers said led us to the airport market, corporate rentals, and other promising markets like truck rentals."

Enterprise insists that most of its success has been driven by listening to its customers and trying to figure out how to respond to their needs. It's how the company got into the car rental business to begin with. Customers asked for replacement vehicles while their cars were in the shop, and that ultimately became part of the business model.

The company also listens closely to its employees. This interaction has opened up many of Enterprise's most successful endeavors, including its customer pick-up service.

Andy Taylor says the reason he built his own office at headquarters with a glass window on the fourth floor—rather than tucked away in a fifth-floor penthouse—is so employees would know he is accessible.

"It was a conscious decision so people would feel free to come up here," he says. "I also go down and eat in our corporate cafeteria on occasion, and people can always come up and talk to me. Every employee has access to my e-mail, so they know they can find me at any time."

Furthermore, Enterprise hires an outside consulting firm to conduct an employee opinion survey every two years. This gives the company a better sense of how workers feel and what areas need improvement. As a result of this feedback, the company has instituted a number of changes to its benefits program, including the implementation of a matching 401(k) plan to enhance the company's retirement benefit.

"You have to treat employees the same way you do customers when talking to them," adds Nicholson. "Just like customers, you need to find out the needs of your employees. It takes listening to them and asking how we can better meet their needs."

"Listening is the only thing that can help us preserve our high standards of personal service and success," adds Andy Taylor. "I challenge every manager to make sure that the ideas of his or her employees are heard and valued."

Strengthen the Community

Andy Taylor likes to think of Enterprise as a local company that just happens to have a presence in thousands of neighborhoods across five countries. "That means we should be on a first-name basis with the people who call these neighborhoods home," he says. "After all, our success depends on their support and goodwill."

The company is determined to be a positive economic force in the communities in which it operates, from St. Louis to the United Kingdom and beyond. Among other things, it purchases millions of dollars worth of vehicles through the local dealerships where it operates, creates hundreds of millions in local tax dollars through sales and employment, and supports thousands of local organizations. It also encourages Enterprise employees to take an active role in their communities.

"We encourage our people and general managers in the field to get involved," Ross says. "We want them to get to know the local culture and find ways to better serve their neighborhoods."

"It's not enough that we're *located* in lots of communities," Andy Taylor insists. "We need to find ways to be more meaningfully *involved* in each community we serve in ways our competitors simply can't match. I've met fascinating people from all walks of life by venturing into the community. It has expanded both our business and my personal horizons. It has opened my mind and allowed me to make a lot of friends. I'd like every employee to have that experience.

"Frankly, some of our competitors cater to gold American Express cardmembers," he continues. "We're not like that, although we're happy to have their business, too. We rent cars to everyone. It's important for us to be well thought of by all of these customers. Since we have a strong relationship in the African-American community, as both an employer and service provider, who better to go on the board of the National Urban League than me? Or why not be active with the United Way and help out the American Red Cross in times of crisis? All of these things help to connect our brand to important stakeholders and more effectively communicate what we stand for."

There is an added business benefit as well. Many CEOs from some of America's largest companies are also on the National Urban League board and various other committees, and all are good connections for the company to make. The same holds true at the branch level, where the city's biggest movers and shakers are well represented on the many local boards Enterprise employees are encouraged to join.

"This kind of service is a great way to broaden your vision and be part of the world, while making important business connections and meeting people who you may not otherwise come to know," Andy Taylor insists.

Service also means offering products that address the needs of the diverse community you work in. As just one example, a group marketing manager in Chicago developed sample rental agreements in both Spanish and Polish to better connect with some of his ethnic customers, who had a hard time reading and understanding the traditional English contracts.

Serving the community extends to those you work with, too. At Enterprise, taking care of employees and their special needs is extremely important.

"Following Hurricane Katrina in New Orleans in 2005, every one of our employees who lived anywhere close opened up their doors to any of their coworkers who lost homes and needed a place to stay," Nicholson notes. "Some of them were still sharing their homes with these employees many months later. We take care of our customers and each other."

Always Keep Your Doors Open

Simply stated, Enterprise believes that its future success depends on its ability to reach out to people of all backgrounds. "This applies to our existing customers, as well as the ones we have yet to win over," Andy Taylor says. "It applies to our current and future employees, and to working with a diverse range of service providers. In other words, our commitment to being an inclusive company extends to every employee, customer, and vendor."

Clearly stating that the company's doors are open to people and ideas of all types is designed to show that it respects the differences that make us all unique. Furthermore, it's a recognition that embracing these differences will help to advance the company's success.

"It really goes back to our brand and what we stand for," Andy Taylor observes. "What are you about? Are you open to ideas, or are you stuck in your own ways of doing things?"

Andy Taylor credits his dad with instilling this belief in him long ago.

"My father has always been a man ahead of his time on all kinds of issues, including race equality," Andy says. "I went to a private high school. At one point, when a person of color decided to enroll, the trustees tried to stop him from being admitted. My father and mother weren't about to let that happen, believing that everyone should be treated the same. They voted to make sure the young man had the right to enter the school. I've always admired that. Today that student is a physician here in St. Louis."

Enterprise has an aggressive recruitment effort to bring more women and minorities into the fold, a recognition that living this value means encouraging and embracing diversity. "We want to match our employee base to the communities we operate in, which means having an open door," says chief operating officer Pam Nicholson.

"The world ahead of us is going to be even more diverse than it is today," Ross insists. "If you aren't looking for things to do in your company in order to excel in this area, you'll fall behind."

Give Back

In the early days of building his business, Jack Taylor admits he didn't think a lot about charity. He was so busy trying to make a living and growing the company, he initially didn't have a lot of money left over. But as he became more secure in his wealth, he realized he wanted to do something more to say thanks to the community for all it had given to him.

"Quite honestly, when you get so much, you ask why you are entitled to all this wealth," Jack says. "I'm having a great time giving money away to things that will improve our communities; our important civic, cultural, and educational institutions; and, as a result, our world."

Enterprise and the entire Taylor family have taken their place among the world's biggest philanthropists. True to its value of strengthening the community one neighborhood at a time, giving back is a strong belief the company holds firm to. It's a mission that began in earnest in 1982 with the forming of the Enterprise Rent-A-Car Foundation.

"The company was doing well, and Dad just decided it was time to start doing something for the communities where we lived and worked," says Jo Ann Taylor Kindle, who now runs the foundation. "He came up with the idea of starting a charitable foundation that is funded out of company profits."

Today, Enterprise sets aside 1.25 percent of companywide pretax profits to fund this endeavor. The foundation takes requests from Enterprise employees, customers, suppliers, and others connected to the company. While all applications are considered when the foundation board meets three times a year, employee requests are almost always granted, assuming the charity they want to support is a recognized nonprofit organization.

"We might not be able to fund the entire amount they ask for, but we will respond to their request," Taylor Kindle says. "Our average gift is between $2,500 and $5,000. We contributed nearly $10 million to almost 700 organizations in 2006."

Over the years, the Enterprise Rent-A-Car Foundation, along with the company and the Taylor family, has given away nearly $200 million. One of the foundation's biggest commitments came in 2006. In honor of the company's upcoming fiftieth anniversary, Enterprise took the unusual step of committing to fund the planting of one million trees a year for the next fifty years in public forests badly in need of reforestation. Enterprise joined with the National Arbor Day Foundation and the National Forest Service to undertake this commitment to improving public lands at a cost of $1 million annually in today's dollars.

"We understand that our business has an impact on the world. This is one way we can give something back in a positive way," says Andy Taylor. "This is also an area close to Jack's heart. He's given $25 million of his own money to the Missouri Botanical Garden for plant categorization in the rain forest of Costa Rica, and another $10 million to the Danforth Plant Science Center for biofuel development." Jack Taylor has also given more than $100 million to leading St. Louis cultural, civic, and educational institutions.

Taylor Kindle oversees the Crawford-Taylor Foundation, which Jack started as well. "He put his five granddaughters on the board with him, because he wants them to understand how all of this works," she says. Members of the Taylor family are huge contributors in their own right and sometimes join forces with the company foundation to coordinate large-scale donations.

Taylor Kindle says that giving back is also good for business— even for those who can only contribute small amounts of money.

"The old model of 'checkbook charity' has evolved into strategic giving programs that tie donations of time, money, and other gifts to defined business goals and desired benefits—while also making sure that gifts are invested in causes that will have a defined positive impact on local communities," she says. "Wouldn't you feel better about doing business with someone who is also doing something for your community? It is not a one-sided deal. That's why it's so important to take care of people in the community."

Consider these statistics: 73 percent of people say they would be more loyal to a business that supports its local community, while 87 percent of workers at companies with philanthropic programs feel a stronger sense of loyalty to their employer. As a national study on the business value of corporate giving by the

Council on Foundations put it, "Products and services surely come first. But corporate America's struggle to earn the loyalties of customers, employees, and shareholders needs more than just high-end quality products and services."

Enterprise also encourages giving by its employees. "Having the foundation is another way to say we want you to get involved and, in turn, we will help to support you," Taylor Kindle says.

"We see a clear connection between our company's health and the health of the communities in which we do business," Andy Taylor adds. "Corporate giving in this case is more than a matter of conscience. It's also a matter of understanding the synergies between our business goals and the goals of the communities where we operate."

Make Core Values More Than Mere Corporate-Speak

Some might dismiss core values as a form of corporate-speak, backed by little serious meaning or passion. That isn't the case at Enterprise.

"First of all, these values are not a temporary, flavor-of-the-month strategy," Andy Taylor insists. "They are a set of guiding principles that will ensure we all have a common point of reference—a behavioral compass, if you will—to help us live the beliefs Jack Taylor set into motion on day one. I can't stress their importance enough. If we want to stay successful, we must agree on these points, and every manager needs to live them and regularly share them with employees."

Andy Taylor is convinced that businesses not taking their core values seriously will suffer the consequences. "These values are the reasons why customers should want to do business with you, why talented people would want to build their careers with you, and why neighbors are glad to have you in their communities," he says. "Whenever we fall short, we give people a reason to go elsewhere."

In giving its employees a card containing the company's founding values that can be carried in their purses or wallets, Enterprise encourages every team member to bring these principles to life for customers and colleagues every day.

"They should constantly ask whether they are living up to the founding values and whether their decisions are in line with what the company stands for," Andy Taylor says. "They need to draw on these values every time they face a tough challenge. By staying focused on them, we improve our work environment and our reputation—which allows us to continue growing our business."

Reward Those Who Exemplify
What You Stand For

When Enterprise set out to recognize those who most fully exemplify the company's founding values, the biggest challenge was figuring out how to measure such intangibles as "strengthening the community" and "keeping the door open." To better gauge how it was doing in each of these areas, Enterprise developed a cultural compass centered on six areas designed to protect the company's greatest asset: its reputation. The points of the compass are Operations, Diversity, Work/Life Balance, Business Practices, Community Relations, Philanthropy, and Government Relations.

To reward exceptional performance, Enterprise created the Jack Taylor Founding Values Award, presented annually to those groups showing the most exceptional performance in all six areas of focus. Winners receive a framed award and a $20,000 grant from the Enterprise Rent-A-Car Foundation to be used to support qualified philanthropic causes in their local communities.

Develop Your Company's Core Values

By now you've discovered the importance of having a values system for your company. So where do you begin the development process? For starters, it needs to originate at the top. Before codifying your culture, ensure that these values are lived and breathed by the company's founder, CEO, and every other executive in the boardroom. If you have a one-person business, it's up to you to carry them out with precision every day. If employees don't see that you are wholeheartedly committed to these ideals, it will be all but impossible to get them on board, no matter what kind of fancy paper you use to print your core values.

With that in mind, and drawing on Enterprise's example, follow these steps to create your company's own list of core values:

1. Determine what makes your business unique and distinct. (If you can't think of anything, address this before going any further.)
2. Make sure your company's values match your own personal beliefs.
3. Let your core values speak loudly about what's most important to you.
4. Use your values to inspire action in your customers and employees.
5. Since core values are constant, be certain your list will stand the test of time.
6. Implement ways to hold everyone accountable to these core values.

7. Clearly define these values, since they will be a critical help when making decisions—particularly for those managers farther down in the organization.

8. Be sure all business strategy and growth objectives stay true to your company's core values.

9. Do everything you can to clearly communicate your core values to everyone in the company on a consistent basis.

How many core values do you need? There really is no magic number. Although Enterprise has eight, some companies have ten or more, while others have only one. You simply need the list to be long enough so that everyone—including your customers and employees—will have a clear understanding of what your company stands for and believes in.

THE   ENTERPRISE   WAY

1. The world's most successful companies live by a clear set of core values.

2. Even if what you stand for is common knowledge, put your core values in writing to ensure that everyone is on the same page.

3. Keep your core values clearly in front of your people and customers at all times, and find ways to make them real.

4. Your core values should reflect what makes your company unique and distinct.

5. There's no magic number of core values you need.

6. Implement ways to hold everyone accountable to following and preserving these values.

7. Make certain that every business decision is guided by your core values.

8. Come up with a way to reward those employees and teams who best exemplify what your company stands for.

9. A key tenet of your core values should be a commitment to give back, in both time and money, to the communities in which you operate.

10. Drawing on Enterprise's example, your core values should include such ideals as listening to your customers, having an open door, rewarding hard work, creating a fun and friendly place to work in, and making customer service a way of life.

Afterword

I F Y O U W E R E to sum up the primary traits that have made Enterprise so successful over the past five decades, it would really come down to the following (and likely in this order):

1. Have a strong belief from the very top that taking care of customers and employees is job number one. Many companies proclaim this in words, but Jack and Andy Taylor (and all other Enterprise officers) actually demonstrate it through their deeds every day. When such a belief emanates from the highest levels of a corporation, it has a tendency to spread like wildfire. Employees can tell whether you really mean what you say, or whether your supposed guiding principles are merely words on paper. Enterprise does more than just talk about good customer service. It has made this commitment a way of life from the top of the company on down. In addition, the company takes pains to ensure that it maintains a powerful—and fun—environment for employees to work in, and one where teamwork always rules.

2. Empower workers as entrepreneurs and pay them on the bottom line. Compensating employees with a fixed salary is fine, but it won't cause them to go above and beyond the call of duty. By sharing a percentage of profits, Enterprise not only brings out the best in its workers, it also causes them to think twice about making unnecessary expenditures and fosters strong loyalty (which translates into high retention). It's important to the company that its employees are empowered to act like owners, and they enjoy the same risks and rewards as entrepreneurs.

3. Hold employees financially accountable for offering excellent customer service. By tracking how satisfied each renter is, Enterprise can determine which workers are best at taking care of customers. As you know, those who fail to wow the company's customers won't get promoted at Enterprise, which limits how much money they can make. In other words, an employee's compensation is tied directly to how well they do at offering excellent customer service.

4. Establish strategic partnerships. There's no question that Enterprise would not be where it is today without the strong alliances it has formed with automobile manufacturers, body shops, car dealerships, and especially insurance companies over the years. By working hard to forge and then maintain these partnerships, Enterprise has earned a significant percentage of the replacement vehicle market. Indeed, if Enterprise were to exist solely on business from its many corporate partners, it would still come close to being America's largest car rental company.

5. Dare to be different. From the way it pays workers to its target market and even office locations, Enterprise has always stood out from the crowd. Instead of fighting for market share with the competition, it opted to serve an entirely different target customer altogether. Rather than paying the traditional low wages of the rental car industry, it chose to reward its managers with generous pay packages. While others sought to increase the number of days cars were out on rental, Enterprise built programs to help its insurance partners actually *reduce* the amount of time customers are without their own vehicles. And as its big competitors struggled financially, Enterprise continued to put up one year of record profitability after another.

The coming decades will no doubt bring many new challenges and opportunities to Enterprise, but sticking to these basic principles will continue to serve the company—and its customers—well. While all of these traits can be adopted by businesses of all types, it's important to remember that execution is everything. You'll need to do more than just make these ideals mere corporate-speak. They must be ingrained into the fabric of your company—and adhered to without fail by everyone from the executive suite on down.

It's a philosophy that Jack Taylor set in motion fifty years ago when he purchased his first seven vehicles, and thus opened the doors to one incredible business.

Acknowledgments

There are so many people who helped to make this book possible, and at the top of the list is Enterprise vice president Patrick Farrell. Pat caught my vision for this book right from the start. He was not only a huge supporter, but also helped to put me in touch with countless Enterprise employees who willingly shared their stories and best practices. I must also thank Ira Robb, a former Enterprise executive who was instrumental in building the company's West Coast operation. Ira introduced me to both Pat and this fabulous organization. I appreciate the trust you two placed in me to tell this great story.

Countless other executives throughout Enterprise graciously talked with me over the course of many months through numerous meetings and follow-up discussions, beginning with founder Jack Taylor and current chairman and CEO Andy Taylor. Together, you two have built an incredible company, and I'm so pleased to know you. Don Ross, Enterprise's president and vice chairman, was another invaluable source of information. Three hours with Don go by like five minutes, as he recounts one fascinating story and business lesson after another. Likewise, chief operating officer Pam Nicholson offered many great insights into the company, including how she was able to rise from management trainee to the fourth-highest-ranking officer in the company in less than two decades. Pam is bound to remain an Enterprise star for many years to come.

While you don't necessarily see all of their names in these pages, my research assistant and co-writer for this project, James Wynbrandt, and I interviewed literally dozens of Enterprise employees for this book. All proved to be helpful sources of information. I'd particularly like to recognize (in alphabetical order) Doug Albrecht, Rick Allen, Marie Artim, Dana Beffa, Ernie Behnke, Van Black, Doug Brown, Lisa Burgess, Jim Burrell, Ruth Carr, Bruce Clifton, Marc Cohn, Christine Conrad, Lanny Dacus, Scott Denson, Lou Galloway, Dan Gass, Rob Hibbard, Susie Irwin, Lee Kaplan, Wayne Kaufman, Craig Kennedy, Jo Ann Taylor Kindle, Rose Langhorst, Bill Lortz, Mary Mahoney, Ed McCarty, Bruce McKee, Jim Mercer, John O'Connell, Carolyn Kindle Payne, Roger Price, Dick Rennecamp, Sandy Rogers, Dave Smith, Steve Smith, Bill Snyder, Greg Stubblefield, Jack Talley, and Chrissy Taylor.

I'd also like to thank Rich Eichwald and Jeff Davis of Fleishman-Hillard, who were terrific sources of information and feedback and provided invaluable assistance in the promotion of this book.

Outside of Enterprise, a number of additional sources proved to be very helpful, including Brian Passell of Progressive and Seth Ingram of Geico. Meanwhile, Linda Cameron and Darla McDavid did an excellent job of transcribing the many hours of interviews conducted with Enterprise executives, and Thomas Perricone provided valuable counsel.

Finally, I must thank Roger Scholl of Doubleday, who is one of the best editors in the business. Roger believed in "The Enterprise Way" from the start, and I can't wait to work with him again. I also appreciate the efforts of the rest of the Doubleday team, including David Drake, Michael Palgon, Meredith McGinnis, Amanda D'Acierno, Sarah Rainone, and Talia Krohn.

Without question, all of you exceeded my expectations as I wrote this book, and I know that together we will help countless other companies learn how they, too, can put employees and customers first, which is bound to lead to big profits.

Index

About the Author

Kirk Kazanjian is the bestselling author of numerous business, investing, and personal finance books. A former award-winning television news anchor and business reporter, he is frequently interviewed by the media and has appeared on CNBC, CNN, Bloomberg, and other radio and television stations across the country. Kazanjian is also a popular speaker and consultant on various business topics, including customer service, management, marketing, employee retention, and branding.

To learn more, or to book Kirk to speak at your company, visit his Web site at www.kirkkazanjian.com. The author also welcomes your feedback at kirk@kirkkazanjian.com.